THE DEATH OF CONSERVATISM

RANDOM HOUSE

NEW YORK

THE DEATH

OF

CONSERVATISM

———

Sam Tanenhaus

Published in the United States by Random House,
an imprint of The Random House Publishing Group,
a division of Random House, Inc., New York.

RANDOM HOUSE and colophon are registered
trademarks of Random House, Inc.

Portions of this work were originally published
in a different form in *The New Republic.*

LIBRARY OF CONGRESS CATALOGING-IN-PUBLICATION DATA
Tanenhaus, Sam.
The death of conservatism / Sam Tanenhaus.
p. cm.
ISBN 978-1-4000-6884-5
eBook ISBN 978-1-58836-948-2
1. Conservatism—United States. I. Title.
JC573.2.U6T355 2009
320.520973—dc22   2009019715

Printed in the United States of America on acid-free paper

www.atrandom.com

2 4 6 8 9 7 5 3 1

FIRST EDITION

Book design by Dana Leigh Blanchette

To my mother,
Gussie Hecht Tanenhaus,
"on whom nothing is lost."

God preserve me from ideologues.

—DANIEL PATRICK MOYNIHAN

Contents

THE DEATH OF CONSERVATISM

1

_____

RIGOR MORTIS

American history is the record, we're often told, of beginnings—dating back to the first settlements planted on the "fresh, green breast of the new world," as F. Scott Fitzgerald wrote in *The Great Gatsby,* his classic tale of self-reinvention. The aura of newness was not merely a sentiment but also a statement of purpose inscribed in our republic's founding documents and asserted in the legend *novus ordo seclorum,* "the new order of the ages," stamped on the Great Seal of the United States.

This ideal has been repeated in an almost unbroken series of rededications of political purpose: Lincoln's "new nation, conceived in Liberty," Theodore Roosevelt's "New Nationalism," Woodrow Wilson's "New Freedom," Franklin D. Roosevelt's "New Deal," John F. Kennedy's "New Frontier," and—circling back to the Great Seal's inscription—George H. W. Bush's "New World Order."

Through all this reinvention runs the theme of American exceptionalism, of a people liberated from the dragging chains of the past.

But of course history is also about endings, and so it has been in America, too. Our cherished myth of continual forward motion rests on dramatic breaks with what came before, whether the suppressions of a state church and the injustices of distant monarchy or our own discarded legacies of slavery and willful isolation from the outside world with its imposition of "entangling alliances."

This cycle of beginnings-in-ends is being repeated again today. We stand on the threshold of a new era that has decisively declared the end of an old one. In the shorthand of the moment this abandoned era is often called the Reagan Revolution. In fact it is something larger and of much longer duration: movement conservatism, the orthodoxy that has been a vital force in our political life for more than half a century and the dominant one during the past thirty years, vanquishing all other rival political creeds until it was itself vanquished in the election of 2008.

This moment's emerging revitalized liberalism has illuminated a truth that should have been apparent a decade ago: movement conservatism is not simply in retreat; it is outmoded. The evidence is not recorded merely in election returns and poll ratings. Those are unreliable and unstable measurements, spontaneous snapshots, subject to sudden change. The more telling evidence is in the realm of ideas and argument. It is there that conservatism is most glaringly disconnected from the realities now besetting America. Even as the collapse of the nation's financial system has driven a nation of 300 million to the brink of the deepest economic crisis since the Great Depression, conservatives remain strangely apart, trapped in the irrelevant causes of another day, deaf to the actual conversation unfolding across the land, in its cities and towns, in red and blue states, in the sanctuaries of the privileged and tented "Bushvilles." This conversation has yielded a new vocabulary—rather, instilled fresh meaning in a familiar vocabulary. It includes phrases like "sensible limits," "sound choices," "shared sacrifice," and "common ideals" and stresses the delicate balance between "mutual obligation" and "individual responsibility." These words, though sometimes vague to the point of abstraction, are firmly anchored in concrete human facts: job layoffs and implausible tuition payments, dwindled savings and parched retirement funds. In aggregate they form the undertone of what Lionel Trilling, in *The Liberal Imagination,* called "a culture's hum and buzz of implication"—a hum and buzz most audible today in gallows humor and nervous asides, in the anxious tones of people, tens of millions if not more, bound in uncertainty and fear, obsessed in their private lives with vast public problems that even "the best and the brightest" seem unable to comprehend, much less solve.

It is all part of an idiom conservatives were once well versed in—and in fact helped create. But today one must strain to hear any semblance of it in the words spoken and written by our professed conservatives, for on the great issues of the day they are virtually silent.

This is not to say conservatives—or what now passes for them—have fallen altogether mute. On the contrary, they continue to intone the stale phrases of movement politics. If you attended a panel luncheon of prominent conservative magazine editors, as I did in the spring of 2009 at the Harvard Club, you heard the urgent call "to take back the culture" (but from whom, exactly?), along with dire admonitions that the Obama administration had placed America's economic "freedom" in jeopardy—this on the very morning that Wall Street had ecstatically embraced the Treasury secretary's plan for assisting the nation's banks.

What these conservative intellectuals said wasn't just mistaken. It was meaningless, the clatter of a bygone period, with its "culture wars" and attacks on sinister "elites." There was no hint of a new argument being formulated or even of an old one being reformulated. More disturbing still, not one of the three panelists acknowledged that the Republican Party and its ideology might bear any responsibility for the nation's current plight. None urged the party and its best thinkers and writers to reexamine their ideas and methods. Each offered instead only the din of ever-loudening distraction, gratingly ill attuned to the conditions of present-day America.

The event was a microcosm of movement conservatism, the corollary of the actions, or rather, inactions, of conservative politicians in the first weeks of the Obama presidency, when Republican legislators marched in virtual lockstep against the stimulus program—even as free-market gurus conceded the federal government must seize command of a ravaged economy; even as Alan Greenspan, a rare penitent on the right, suggested we might need to nationalize failing banks; even as Republican governors and mayors clamored for precisely the rescue Democrats fashioned, however imperfectly, not for the purpose of creating a newly socialized state, but to keep people in their jobs, to keep schools and hospitals functioning and families from losing their homes.

How did the GOP and its intellectual allies sink into this torpor? One answer is complacency. For many years the Right, in its position of dominance, felt no need to think hard, least of all about itself. Another is that the crisis on the right is the endgame of a long-running debate—not only between conservatism and liberalism, but also *within* conservatism, and sometimes within the minds of individual conservatives—about the nature of government and society, and about the role of politics in binding the two. At its vibrant best, this debate, initially limited to a small group of thinkers and writers, energized the Republican Party and then ramified outward to become a broader quarrel that shaped, and at times defined, the political stakes of several generations.

In those earlier times—as long ago as the 1950s and as recently as the 1980s—conservative arguments, while expressed through politics, spoke to the deepest issues of culture and society. This is no longer the case. Instead, we hear exhortations *from* the Right *to* the Right: to uphold "basics" and "principles," to stand tall against liberals—even if it means evading the most pressing issues of the moment. Today's conservatives resemble the exhumed figures of Pompeii, trapped in postures of frozen flight, clenched in the rigor mortis of a defunct ideology.

Of course conservatism has fallen on hard times before—and been declared dead—only to translate presumed defeats into starting points for future triumph. In 1954, the movement's first national tribune, Senator Joseph McCarthy, was checkmated by the Eisenhower administration and then "condemned" by his Senate colleagues. But the episode, and the passions it aroused, led to the founding of *National Review*, the movement's first serious political journal. Ten years later, the Right's next leader, Barry Goldwater, suffered one of the most lopsided losses in election history. Yet the "Draft Goldwater" campaign secured control of the GOP for movement conservatives. In 1976, the challenge by Goldwater's heir Ronald Reagan to the incumbent president, Gerald Ford, fell short. But the crusade positioned Reagan to win the presidency four years later and initiate the conservative "revolution" that remade our politics over the next quarter century. In each instance, crushing defeat gave the movement new strength and pushed it farther along the route to ultimate victory. In each instance, too, conservatives could argue—and did, with persuasive eloquence—that their vision had not been rejected so much as denied the opportunity to be tested.

Today it is impossible to make this case. During the two terms of George W. Bush, conservative ideas were not merely tested but also pursued with dogmatic fixity, though few conservatives will admit it, just as few seem ready to think honestly about the consequences of a presidency that failed not because it "betrayed" movement ideology but because it often enacted that ideology so rigidly: the aggressively unilateralist foreign policy; the blind faith in a deregulated, Wall Street–centric market; the harshly punitive "culture war" waged against liberal enemies. That these precepts should have found their final, hapless defender in John McCain, who had contested them for most of his long career, only confirms that movement doctrine retains an inflexible and suffocating grip on the Republican Party and its most vocal advocates.

Yet there is no sign that movement stalwarts are ready to give any of this up. Some concede the Democrats are now in command and have in Barack Obama a leader of rare political skills. Some admit further that the specific failures of the outgoing administration were legion.

But what of the verdict issued on movement conservatism itself? There, conservatives have offered little apart from self-justifications mixed with shallow appraisals of the Bush years. Some argue that the administration wasn't conservative at all, at least not in the "small government" sense. This is true, but then no president in modern times, Democrat or Republican, has seriously attempted to reduce the size of government, and for good reason: voters don't want it reduced. What they want is government that's "big" for them—whether it's Democrats who call for job-training programs and universal health care or Republicans eager to see billions funneled into "much-needed and underfunded defense procurement," as William Kristol recommended shortly after Obama's victory.

Others on the right blame Bush's heterodoxy on interlopers, chief among them Kristol's band of warriors at *The Weekly Standard*, who beguiled the administration into the Iraq war and an ill-starred Wilsonian crusade for global democracy. But here again the facts are complicated: Bush's foreign policy was indeed developed in part by neoconservatives convinced that American-style democracy can be imposed on distant lands. But it derived equally from the hard-line anti-Communist philosophy developed in the first years of the Cold War. "Paleoconser-

vatives" deplored the overly "defensive" posture of the containment policies developed by Presidents Truman and Eisenhower,
with its emphasis on carefully managed alliances like NATO and
the "economic diplomacy" of the Marshall Plan; later they opposed arms treaties and nuclear test bans, pressing instead for
a more confrontational "liberationist" or "rollback" approach
that might include "limited" nuclear war. This ardent militarism
underlay Goldwater's call in his 1960 manifesto, *The Conscience
of a Conservative*, for a foreign policy "primarily offensive in nature," honed to meet "the dynamic, revolutionary character of
the enemy's challenge" and prepared "to engage the enemy at
times and places, and with weapons, of our own choosing."

Bush drew on this history when he announced a preemptive
war against Islamic jihadists, asserting that "Cold War doctrines
of deterrence and containment" must now be replaced by a
strategy of prevention that enables us to "take the battle to the
enemy, disrupt his plans, and confront the worst threats before
they emerge." The trouble, as some recognized at the time, was
that the administration was reviving rhetoric formulated during
a period of bipolar conflict in the belief, or faith, that it could be
applied to the profoundly dissimilar threats posed by a loose fed-
eration of terrorist groups.

Some critics on the right say the fault lay not with the administration's goals but with its incompetent strategies and execution, and perhaps with Bush's own rigid character. But a principal
lesson of modern American politics, learned or not learned time
and again, is that ideas and execution are inextricably bound.
What a president seeks to do inevitably determines how he does
it. If he's an ideologue, ideology will influence decisions made
at every level of government, from the appointment of federal

judges, cabinet officials, and top White House advisers to the mid-level staffing of obscure agencies, from the conceptualization of global strategies and big-picture "guidances" to the drafting of specific policy provisions.

For others on the right the issue is primarily one of defective marketing. In their view, America remains a center-right nation as persuaded as ever by movement dogma. The Republicans might well have captured the 2008 election had Karl Rove and his team of operatives not grown complacent after their victories in 2002 and 2004 and failed to update "the brand" to suit changing demographics in Sunbelt states like Colorado and Nevada, with their socially liberal white professionals and economically liberal blue-collar Hispanics. But this thesis evades a big question: What does the movement have to offer such constituencies apart from a plea for their votes?

Even now, movement activists seem less intent on thinking through these questions than on stockpiling ammunition for the next election, convinced they will win if the Democrats stumble often enough or if the economy continues to worsen. This is what lurks beneath the hope, widespread on the right and voiced most openly by Rush Limbaugh, that Obama's policies will fail. Limbaugh's remarks were widely condemned (though the White House gleefully seized on them as further proof of the movement's appetite for destruction). Conservative politicians, at once alarmed by Limbaugh and fearful of him, twisted themselves into pained contortions of obeisance and reproof. But in strategic terms Limbaugh was acknowledging, however crudely, the heliocentrism of our two-party system as it has evolved over the past century and a half, an extended period characterized by long cycles—roughly thirty to thirty-six years—

of one-party dominance. "Thumbing back through history," the political journalist Samuel Lubell wrote in his classic *The Future of American Politics*, "we find relatively few periods when the major parties were closely competitive, with elections alternating between one and the other. The usual pattern has been that of a dominant majority party, which stayed in office as long as its elements held together, and a minority party which gained power only when the majority coalition split. Our political solar system, in short, has been characterized not by two equally competing suns, but by a sun and a moon. It is within the majority party that the issues of any particular period are fought out; while the minority party shines in reflected radiance of the heat thus generated."

Conservatives today face a choice: Will they shine in reflected radiance or spin futilely on their lonely unlit orbit? If they seriously mean to offer more than nihilism, they must accept the obligation history places on the party exiled from power: the obligation to rethink and reevaluate, to undergo the serious work of self-examination and preparation.

Conservatives did exactly that during the long period that extended from the 1930s through the 1960s, a "down" cycle that prefigured this current one. At first many on the right, like Rush Limbaugh today, promulgated the dogmas of grievance and resentment, insisting in words like Limbaugh's own that "the enemy within" had committed "treason" against the United States.

But the movement's best thinkers grew to understand that such denunciations amounted to a denunciation of America itself. They chose instead to address the authentic, rather than invented, crises of their time and tried to fashion serious rather than merely expedient arguments. They became analysts and critics, theorists and prophets. They observed politics from an engaged, constructive distance, made their outer orbit a useful vantage point from which to calibrate where the nation, under liberal rule, might be headed. And they exerted whatever influence they could through the vehicles of ideas and arguments. Unwelcome in "the mainstream media," they could easily have retreated into an alternative universe and limited their conversation to preachments aimed at the like-minded few. They rejected that course, electing instead to seize whatever openings they could to join the larger quarrels, adapting their voices to the idioms and vocabulary of the day. When at last conservatives gained a foothold within the establishment, political and intellectual, it was because they had earned their way. They rejected extremism for centrism, purism for pragmatism, revanchism for realism. The public—including much of the liberal public—deemed them ready to govern. The moon had become a sun.

Are conservatives prepared to travel this route again? No, to judge from current evidence. The figures now contending for movement leadership—Limbaugh; the GOP's new Lazarus, Newt Gingrich; the aspirant governors Bobby Jindal and Sarah Palin—seem contentedly nestled within their fringe orbit. Even when they speak of reclaiming the center, they do so in the discredited idioms of the discarded past. This is equally true of the movement's intelligentsia. Journals like *Commentary*, *National Review*, and *The Weekly Standard*, once sophisticated publications, are now mouthpieces of the Republican Party at its most revanchist. During the 2008 campaign one could read—at times scarcely avoid—effusions like those of Michael Barone inveighing against "the coming Obama thugocracy" and Jonah Goldberg railing against Obama's "pals from the Weather Underground who murdered or celebrated the murder of policemen." Most unsettling of all, perhaps, was the case of William Kristol, the founding publisher and editor of *The Weekly Standard*, who in his election-year column for *The New York Times* debased this valued space into a shabby storefront for the Republican presidential campaign. These conservative intellectuals recognize no distinction between analysis and advocacy, or between the competition of ideas and the naked struggle for power. To them the Democratic Party and all manner of liberals are simply the enemy, and if the majority of the country joins the "wrong" side, then they are the enemy, too, or its manipulated pawns.

All movements have life spans. They spring into existence in response to particular conditions, and when those conditions change, often as a result of movement successes, they either disband or lose their relevance. The abolitionist movement effectively ended once Lincoln signed the Emancipation Proclamation. The progressive movement lasted only fifteen years (from 1900 to 1915), but in that time transformed American politics, shaping two of the great twentieth-century presidencies, Theodore Roosevelt's and Woodrow Wilson's, and making possible a third, Franklin D. Roosevelt's.

In more recent times, too, movements have forcefully shaped our politics: the civil rights movement of the 1950s and 1960s; the feminist movement of the 1970s; the evangelical movement of the 1980s; the environmentalist movement, born in the 1960s and just now reaching its peak influence. All were social movements that eventually found political outlets. But of all American movements, only ideological conservatism was from its inception explicitly political—that is to say, preoccupied with the question of power (how to obtain it, how to wield it, how to keep it)—to the exclusion, at times, of all other considerations.

This explains the air of embattlement that has so often characterized the American Right, even when it has attained power at the highest levels of government and society. Of the last six Republican presidents, three (Nixon, Reagan, and George W. Bush) had strong ties to movement conservatism, while three others (Eisenhower, Ford, George H. W. Bush) did not. The differences between the two groups had less to do with policy than with politics. The first three pursued a revanchist course in which institutional conflicts—waged against the other branches of government or against the "permanent government" of the executive—were part of a broader ideological campaign too urgent to be trusted to the traditional channels of governance. This resulted in breaches of conduct widely deemed illegal—and even impeachable (Watergate, Iran-contra, various aspects of "the war on terror"). In contrast, "merely" Republican leaders from Eisenhower to the first Bush respected the established boundaries of constitutional precedent, even if it meant carrying out actions imposed by hostile congressional majorities and adversarial courts.

In his essay "The Civil Rights Movement and the Coming Constitutional Crisis," the conservative political thinker Willmoore Kendall noted that adherents of revolutionary movements, right and left, can be described as people who "will not take No for an answer." This adamant refusal is the essence of movement conservatism, which is not to say right-wing ideologues invariably champion a strong or "imperial" presidency. Sometimes they do, but only when one of their own occupies the office. During Democratic and even moderately Republican presidencies, movement conservatives have waged destructive campaigns led within Congress, whether it has been Senator Joseph McCarthy's "investigations" of the Truman and Eisenhower administrations or Newt Gingrich and Tom DeLay's orchestration of Bill Clinton's impeachment.

Therein lies the paradox of the modern Right. Its drive for power has steered it onto a path that has become profoundly and defiantly *un*-conservative—in its arguments and ideas, in its tactics and strategies, above all in its vision.

What we call conservatism today would have been incomprehensible to the great originator of modern conservatism, Edmund Burke, who in the late eighteenth century set forth the principles by which governments might nurture the "organic" unity that bound a people together even in times of revolutionary upheaval. Burke's conservatism was based not on a particular set of ideological principles but rather on distrust of *all* ideologies, beginning with their totalizing nostrums. In his most celebrated work, *Reflections on the Revolution in France* (1790), a series of bulletins on the insurrectionists and their English supporters, Burke made no sustained effort to justify the ancien régime and its many "abuses." Nor did he propose a counter-ideology. Instead, he warned against the destabilizing perils of extremist politics of any kind. The Jacobins—in particular Robespierre, who proclaimed a "despotism of liberty"— and more moderate figures, too, were inflamed with the

Enlightenment vision of the ideal civilization and sacrificed to its abstractions the established traditions and institutions of what Burke called "civil society." With "the delusive plausibilities of moral politicians," they placed an idea of the perfect society over and above the need to improve society as it really existed. They deemed France "incapable or undeserving of reform, so that it was of absolute necessity the whole fabric should be at once pulled down, and the area cleared for the erection of a theoretic experimental edifice in its place."

To Burke, "political reason is a computing principle," a matter of "adding, subtracting, multiplying, and dividing," the emphasis on continual adjustment and recalibration of the existing order. This, in turn, meant governments were obligated to use their powers to meliorate intolerable conditions. Thus, though an ardent defender of the English political system of his day, which severely limited suffrage, Burke had nonetheless sympathized with the American Revolution. This seemed contradictory but was not, for the architects of colonial independence, unlike the French rebels, didn't seek to destroy the English government; on the contrary, they regarded themselves as faithful adherents of English law and justly accused England of having violated its own political and legal traditions by unlawfully imposing measures like the Stamp Act without allowing the colonists to make their dissenting case in Parliament. Burke, as it happened, opposed the colonists' plea for parliamentary representation—because they practiced slavery, to Burke an intolerable offense. "Common sense, nay self-preservation," he wrote, "seem to forbid, that those, who allow themselves an unlimited right over the liberties and lives of others, should have any share in making laws for those, who have long renounced such unjust and cruel distinctions." Even so, Burke recognized the legitimacy of the rebels' grievance. More practically, he weighed the costs of their growing estrangement from the motherland. "He was trying, during the early phases of the pre-revolutionary process, to persuade the English not to provoke Americans into rebellion," Conor Cruise O'Brien writes in *The Great Melody*, his "thematic biography" of Burke. "During the later pre-revolutionary phases, he was trying to dissuade the English from using force against the Americans; during the actual revolutionary war he was trying, with little hope up to 1778, and no success up to 1782, to persuade the English to concede independence to the Americans; *de facto* independence up to 1778; *de jure* independence from then on." Instead, George III stubbornly clung to the hard line and so shared responsibility for the uprising when it came. "A state without the means of some change is without the means of its conservation," Burke warned. The task of statesmen was to maintain equilibrium between "the two principles of conservation and correction." To govern was to engage in perpetual compromise— "sometimes between good and evil, and sometimes between evil and evil." In such a scheme there is no useful place for the either/or of ideological purism.

In her study *On Revolution*, Hannah Arendt, following Burke, contrasted the American and the French models. The first was conservative because it accepted normative political tradition. Its leaders were "eager to preserve what ha[d] been done [previously] and to assure its stability rather than open for new things, new developments, new ideas." The Bill of Rights, for instance, was "meant to institute permanent restraining controls upon all political power, and hence presupposed the existence of a body politic and the functioning of political power." In contrast, the

French rebels wanted to alter the relationship between men and politics. The "Rights of Man" propounded by the French "were meant to spell out primary positive rights, inherent in man's nature, as distinguished from his political status, and as such they tried indeed to reduce politics to nature." Robespierre and company had "no respect for the legal personality which is given and guaranteed by the body politic." It was no surprise, then, that the Reign of Terror "eventually spelled the exact opposite of true liberation and true equality."

The movement conservatives of our time seem the heirs of the French rather than of the American Revolution. They routinely demonize government institutions, which they depict as the enemy of the people's best interests. But to classical conservatives the two entities, government and society, are mutually dependent. Burke drew no meaningful distinction between the state and society—that is, between the formally established institutions of government and those institutions rooted in patrimony, custom, and habit. The two were coterminous, at times almost interchangeable. "Government is a contrivance of human wisdom to provide for human *wants*," he wrote, adding a few sentences later, as if following a single arc of thought, "Society requires not only that the passions of individuals should be subjected, but that even in the mass and body as well as in the individuals, the inclinations of men should frequently be thwarted, their will controlled, and their passions brought into subjection. This can only be done *by a power out of themselves* . . . [T]he restraints on men, as well as their liberties, are to be reckoned among their rights. But as the liberties and the restrictions vary with times and circumstances, and admit of infinite modifications, they cannot be settled upon any abstract rule."

To read Burke and Arendt is to realize how far "the movement" has strayed from genuinely conservative ideals. Today it is almost taken for granted that the American Right is intrinsically hostile to both governmental *and* social institutions, seeing in each a purveyor of false values that imperil the "true America."

The story of postwar American conservatism is best understood as a continual replay of a single long-standing debate. On one side are realists who have upheld the Burkean ideal of replenishing civil society by adjusting to changing conditions. On the other are revanchists committed to a counterrevolution, whether the restoration of America's pre–New Deal ancien régime, the return to Cold War–style Manichaeanism, or the revival of premodern "family values." Like most such categories, realism and revanchism are not neatly divisible. Their adherents do not storm onto the political battlefield clad in different uniforms. Instead, these terms indicate poles between which the movement constantly oscillates, now pushing closer to one end of the continuum, now the other.

But it is also the case that at almost every critical juncture, the revanchists have won the argument. They have done so by perfecting a politics energized by Jacobin-like marshalings of shared enmity. Oppositionism is a powerful tool. It can bridge differences among groups otherwise at odds. Wall Street tycoons and Wal-Mart shoppers, authoritarian evangelicals and libertarian antitax brigades, "America First" isolationists and "unipolar" internationalists—all have been brought together in a unity of certitude that liberalism violates and even subverts

American interests and values. It was this belief that bound the Right's factions during the movement's zenith from the 1980s to the 2000s, until the crises of the Bush years drove them centripetally apart, sending both the Republican Party and its allies on their lonely marginal orbit. Even now, conservatives still insist theirs is the party of true ideological diversity, more inclusive than the Democratic Party's unruly coalition of "interest groups."

But there is a fundamental difference between the two parties and the politics that guides them. The modern liberal worldview is premised on consensus. Movement conservatism emphasizes orthodoxy. In his pioneering essay "The Convenient State" (1961), the twenty-six-year-old Garry Wills, at the time the most promising young conservative thinker in America, clarified the distinction: "A consensus, as the word's form indicates, is a meeting of several views on common ground; an orthodoxy is the reduction of all views to a single view. Consensus implies compromise, establishing a minimal ground of agreement on which to base political organization. Orthodoxy goes to the roots of metaphysical and religious awareness and demands a 'right view' on these things, not merely a *modus vivendi*. (The contemporary word for this is 'ideology.')" These distinctions still define our politics. Liberals place faith in the interrelated processes of politics and governance. Conservatives subordinate governance to politics and ideological certitude—or, in the Catholic formulation favored by some conservatives, to *recta ratio*, "right reason."

Practically, this vision of orthodoxy amounts to war fought by other means. This was the argument put forth by Kendall, a disillusioned ex-Trotskyist who emerged as one of the Right's most fertile thinkers during the Cold War period. His essay

"What Is Conservatism?," published in 1963, drew a bright line of demarcation between the Left and the Right. "The line in question is a *line of battle*," Kendall wrote, "a line of battle moreover in *contemporary American politics* and a line of battle between two sets of *combatants*, each fighting to *defeat* the other."

Since liberals at the time held the advantage, conservatives were obligated to resist. And since they were removed from power, their primary means were rhetorical. As Kendall's disciple William F. Buckley Jr. put it: "Rhetoric is the principal thing. It precedes all action." This was written in 1967, the same year one of the most astute liberals of the period, Richard N. Goodwin, observed that "conservatives seem to have a genius for winning the all-important semantic battles. Anti-union laws become 'right to work'; national health insurance becomes 'socialized medicine'; a proposal to eliminate the concentration of the draft on the poor and disadvantaged becomes a 'lottery.' " And, Goodwin noted, "those who oppose such policies are often cast by this brilliant rhetorical device as betrayers of the national interest."

This vocabulary has changed remarkably little in forty years. As if by atavistic reflex, conservative opponents of Barack Obama have applied the epithet "socialism" to his ambitious plans to exert greater federal control over health care and energy policy, even though the Bush administration, the most conservative in modern history, itself orchestrated a $700 billion bailout of Wall Street, the Troubled Assets Relief Program (TARP). After Obama's first address to a joint session of Congress, in February 2009, Charles Krauthammer warned, in his *Washington Post* column, that Obama is exploiting "the current crisis . . . to move the still (relatively) modest American welfare state toward European-style social democracy." And Newt Gingrich warned that Obama's budget amounted to "European socialism transplanted to Washington."

The politics of consensus would have required Krauthammer and Gingrich to acknowledge an inescapable fact: the public favored Obama's proposals. But the politics of orthodoxy imposes no such obligation. "Right reason" makes no allowances for public opinion, because the public is so often wrong. Yet this approach is radically at odds with how democracy really works, with its intricately managed modus vivendi. "Public opinion is a permeating influence, and it exacts obedience to itself," Walter Bagehot wrote in "The Character of Sir Robert Peel," his classic essay on statesmanship, published in 1856. "Those who desire a public career must look to the views of the living public . . . You cannot, many people wish you could, go into parliament to represent yourself. You must conform to the opinions of the electors."

The primary dynamic of American politics, normally described as a continual friction between the two major parties, is equally in our time a competition between the liberal idea of consensus and the conservative idea of orthodoxy. We see it in the Democratic Party's recent history of choosing centrist, explicitly non-ideological presidential candidates (Kennedy, Johnson, Carter, Clinton, Obama), as contrasted with the Republicans' preference for ideologically committed ones (Goldwater, Reagan, George W. Bush).

The struggle between consensus and orthodoxy illuminates as well the contrasting approaches favored by each party's congressional caucus. When Ronald Reagan took office in 1981, he presented a program of steep tax cuts that many Democrats found radical. Yet forty-eight Democrats in the House and thirty-seven in the Senate voted for it. They did so partly in acknowledgment of the sweeping victory Reagan had won—51 percent of the vote, less than Obama won in 2008, but ten points more than the Democratic incumbent, Jimmy Carter, got. Still, Democrats had a fifty-vote advantage in the House in 1981. They could have stopped Reagan—or at least made a strong case for opposing him. Instead, they deferred to the popular will and to the tradition of allowing a new president to pursue his agenda.

A more striking example came in 2001. George W. Bush lost the popular vote, and there was an outcry after the Supreme Court intervened to halt the Florida recount. Yet Democrats made no serious effort to block Bush's major initiatives.

Contrast this with the example of Bill Clinton after his election in 1992. It is often remarked that Clinton was thwarted in major efforts—for instance, health care reform—because he failed to win more than 50 percent of the vote, thanks to the third-party presence of H. Ross Perot. "He didn't get a majority," the top Republican senator, Bob Dole, said once the returns were counted. The country, he added, "had plenty of doubts about Clinton. They want change. Well, we want to be responsible and deliver change, whatever that means, but we're skeptical so we'll wait and see."

In fact, Clinton's victory was decisive. He defeated George H. W. Bush by five percentage points (Obama, without the impediment of a serious third-party challenge, defeated McCain by seven). And Clinton captured a bigger share than Obama of the electoral college. More important, the 38 percent total of the popular vote Bush received was lower than Carter's total in 1980—in fact, lower than Herbert Hoover's in 1932, amid the cataclysm of the Great Depression. Clinton had compared Bush to Hoover a month before Election Day, when the Census Bureau reported that nearly thirty-six million Americans were living below the poverty line, a greater number than at any time since 1964, the year Lyndon Johnson declared "war" on poverty.

Once in office, Clinton, again like Obama, quickly proposed an economic stimulus program, a modest $19.5 billion jobs bill. It seemed likely to pass. Democrats had achieved congressional majorities in both houses almost identical in size to those they hold now. But Dole mustered his Republican minority to enforce a filibuster—four times—and the original bill never reached a vote. A version did finally pass, but it had been stripped to a skeletal $4 billion.

Dole's use of the filibuster was a sharp break with legislative precedent, "a troubling and deepening failure of the Republican Party to play within the established constitutional rules," Alan Ehrenhalt, the editor of *Governing,* the respected nonpartisan journal, wrote when he revisited the episode in 1999. "It is true that the filibuster has a long and disreputable Senate history and that, over the years, it has been used more by Democrats than by Republicans. But only after 1992 did it become the centerpiece of opposition conduct toward an elected President. What the Republicans did in the Senate in 1993 amounted to an unreported constitutional usurpation." But to Dole it looked very different. He was the appointed guardian of the movement, charged to assert its ideology, its "fundamental difference of philosophy" with the new president—and the plurality of voters who elected him.

As it happened, the Republicans were vindicated. The recession cycle had all but ended by the time Clinton took office, and the economy rebounded. Clinton, recognizing this, adjusted course and oversaw a period of remarkable prosperity. Unemployment decreased in each of the eight years he was in office. Like Dwight Eisenhower forty years before, he was a genuine Burkean. Both presidents struggled to neutralize movement forces in Congress through "a computing principle." Both succeeded. And both left office with soaring approval ratings. They are the modern era's two true conservative presidents—and the two best.

Barack Obama began his presidency amid conditions much grimmer than those in 1993 but also with advantages Clinton lacked. He captured a majority of the popular vote, and once he was in office, his popularity grew, owing partly to the country's excitement at having elected its first black president, partly to the widespread belief that the Republicans were to blame for the economic collapse that had secured Obama's victory. Yet House Republicans, the last organized enclave of movement politics, held fast to their revanchist position and duplicated the resistance tactics of 1993. Not one Republican House member voted for Obama's stimulus bill, though it included numerous concessions in the form of tax cuts. And only three Republican senators supported it. One of the three, Arlen Specter, later switched parties. The "line of battle" remained sharp. Orthodoxy overrode consensus; the ideologues disdained the modus vivendi.

To liberals, or many of them, the decay of conservatism is a welcome development, and long overdue—a matter not of decline but of the truth finally emerging. For these the Right has been from its inception stained with the darkest legacies of the American character—narrow-mindedness, provincialism, anti-intellectualism, coldheartedness, bigotry—and its ascendancy has been a continual narrative of reactionary or rearguard actions. But this view overlooks the vital contributions conservatism has made over the decades and overlooks whole areas of American life that for many years the Right understood better than the Left. Norman Mailer recognized this in 1968, the year the conservative sun first eclipsed the liberal moon. "The Left was years away from a vision sufficiently complex to give life to the land," Mailer wrote in *Miami and the Siege of Chicago,* his account of that year's two political conventions. "The Left had not yet learned to talk across the rugged individualism of the more rugged in America."

Today, it is not so easy to separate the more rugged from the less. We all stand in more or less the same place. The old battles have been fought to a meaningless draw, the fate most such battles usually meet. Liberals, after a long period in the wilderness, now seem to understand by and large that American politics is a replenishing exercise in adjustment and accommodation. It is the same lesson conservatives absorbed long ago, when their movement was most vital. It is the lesson they need to learn again.

2

___

OLD BOLSHEVIKS AND
YOUNG RADICALS

W hy has movement conservatism pursued so destructive a course? Why has it depended for so long on a politics of enmity, of polarizing divisiveness rather than common concerns? Why does the contemporary Right define itself less by what it yearns to conserve than by what it longs to destroy: "statist" social programs; "socialized medicine"; "big labor"; "activist" Supreme Court justices; the "media elite"; "tenured radicals" on university faculties; "experts" in and out of government?

The answer lies in the origins of the modern Right, which came into existence during the great liberal experiments of the New Deal.

Much has been written lately about this period, and for good reason, since it closely parallels our own. The emphasis has been on New Deal policy—the boldly regulatory measures Franklin D. Roosevelt took to tame the furies of a ravaged economy through the proliferation of federal agencies and programs: the Agricultural Adjustment Administration, the Securities and Exchange Commission, the National Labor Relations Board, and all the rest, capped by the Social Security Act.

Today it is generally understood that Roosevelt was improvising solutions to a crisis that required immediate action, not least since a fearful public was clamoring for it. But at the time his solutions struck many as extreme—not just because of what the New Deal did but also because of who was doing it. "Roosevelt had quickly seen that he could not fight the depression through the Departments of Agriculture, Labor, Commerce and the Treasury (or, later, fight the war through State, War and Navy)," Arthur Schlesinger Jr. wrote in his book *A Thousand Days*. "He had therefore bypassed the traditional structure, resorting instead to the device of the emergency agency, set up outside the civil service and staffed from top to bottom by men who believed in New Deal policies." A good example of the new kind of government figure was Adolf A. Berle, a professor of economic law at Columbia, whose book *The Modern Corporation and Private Property*, published during the 1932 election, became a doctrinal source of New Deal fiscal policy. Drawing on statistics provided by the economist Gardiner Means, Berle carefully anatomized the "corporate revolution" that had transferred "perhaps two-thirds of the industrial wealth of the country from individual ownership to ownership by the large, publicly financed corporations," which in turn had "vitally change[d]" the lives of owners, laborers, and consumers. Nothing less than "a new form of economic organization of society," this "silent revolution" posed "the problem of the relation which the corporation will ultimately bear to the state—whether it will dominate the state or be regulated by the state or whether the two will coexist with relatively little connection. In other words, as between a political organization of society and an economic organization of society which will be the dominant form?" In effect, the New Deal was created to answer this question—to strike the optimum balance between economics and politics.

It made sense that Berle, with his acute technical grasp of corporations and credit, should find his way to Washington and join Roosevelt's brain trust. But his presence there was a novelty. "We were freaks—like phrenologists," he later said. "A politician who talked to a professor in those days kept it a deep, dark secret."

America prized its men of action—its frontiersmen and practical inventors. Its ethos of rugged individualism championed the free market, a holdover from the Gilded Age, when industrialism had created a new class of plutocrats who formed the nation's true elite and formulated its regnant system of moral values: self-interest, self-motivation, belief in the autarkic splendors of the market. Some insisted the problems were providential. "The financial community purported to see the depression as a blessed occurrence which would improve the national character by chastening the spirit," William E. Leuchtenburg notes in his book *The Perils of Prosperity.* "Even hard-shelled British Tories were shocked by the resistance of American businessmen to unemployment insurance."

That the nation should turn to professors in its time of trouble was an affront, a confession of weakness. To an intellectual like H. L. Mencken, the figure who presided over this change was, variously, a "dictator," "chartered libertine," and the "King in the White House." Roosevelt really believed, to Mencken's astonishment, that "the nation would be vastly benefited if its present scheme of government could be radically overhauled, and the safeguards now thrown about property eliminated, and all power and prerogative handed over to men of vision, sworn to serve and save the lowly." In fact, the New Deal was "a political racket . . . and nothing more," Mencken wrote on the eve of the 1936 election. "Its chief practical business is to search out groups that can be brought into the [Democratic Party] machine by grants out of the public treasury, which is to say, out of the pockets of the rest of us."

This argument, in one version or another, was elaborated by other Old Right intellectuals—the "Tory anarchist" Albert Jay Nock (author of *Our Enemy, the State*), the *Saturday Evening Post* business writer Garet Garrett (who deplored the growing autonomy of labor unions), the proto-libertarian Frank Chodorov (*The Income Tax: Root of All Evil*). Their names are barely remembered today. But they were the first authentic voices of movement conservatism, its overtones still audible in recent books like Jonah Goldberg's *Liberal Fascism* and Amity Shlaes's *The Forgotten Man*. It is a politics of accusatory protest. Elected officials practice it, too—for instance, Ron Paul, the Texas congressman who attained cult status during the 2008 Republican campaign and then, during Obama's first days in office, declared at the Conservative Political Action Conference: "We now have moved a major step in the direction of socialism. We are close to a fascist system where the government has control of our lives and our economy."

As it happened, Roosevelt's ambitions did reach outsize proportions—first, following his massive reelection victory in 1936, when he violated "the unwritten Constitution" in his botched attempt to pack the Supreme Court by increasing the number of justices to fifteen, the new appointees meant to overrule the conservatives, who had thwarted so many New Deal programs; then when he decided to seek a third term in 1940, setting off fierce debate and renewed charges of demagoguery. Even some cankered Democrats banded to oppose him, including Roosevelt's onetime mentor Al Smith, who scathingly denounced the "indispensable man."

In a nationwide radio address from Columbus, Ohio, two weeks before Election Day 1940, Herbert Hoover, who for years had been warning that "the New Deal party" was joining the global "march to socialism," pushed the analogy further. Just as "the Nazi party rules Germany, the Communist party rules Russia, the Fascist party rules Italy," Hoover said, so Roosevelt "has builded [sic] personal power to a dangerous point" through his rapid and vast expansion of the executive branch. "They have mobilized about 1,500,000 Federal and State officials who are allied with the New Deal party," Hoover estimated, and these officials were running a colossal patronage operation. "The great shower of manna which must or may be rained on one-third of our unfortunate homes through relief, subsidies or government contracts" was controlled by "a department of machine politics," which manipulated the will of pliant voters. "There can be no free election," Hoover predicted, as long as "ten million households" were umbilically attached to Roosevelt's party. And suppose he did indeed win a third term? Might it not "lead to a political machine which can elect to a fourth term or even a life term"? Also: "Under assumptions of personal power we are steadily drifting toward war." All this was more or less true. Roosevelt won in 1940 and led the country into World War II. He ran again as a war president in 1944, and died shortly into his fourth term.

Hoover's attack on the New Deal was not explicitly ideological or even partisan. It derived in part from the progressive crusade of the early 1910s, when advocates of sound government and civic virtue battled big-city bosses dispensing Tammany-style patronage. But FDR was himself an heir to the progressives. The "shower of manna" wasn't a payoff. It was a lifeline—the supply of "wants" Burke had said government was obligated to provide.

The Old Right's attacks on the New Deal masked a deeper anxiety about changes overtaking America, no longer a pastoral land of rural communities and small towns, with their cracker-barrel politics, but an urbanized industrial nation with ever-more-complex constituencies—teeming ethnic populations in northern cities, increasingly organized and disciplined labor unions.

The Right had no answer to this. Hoover still called himself a liberal, a proponent of "ordered liberty," based on "open and equal opportunity." The New Deal represented "a false liberalism that substitutes government of men for government of laws" and imposed "a planned economy" whose heavy tax burden and collectivist vision reduced working citizens to "slavery." The protest was genuine, and at times persuasive. But in the end it offered little beyond grievance and the consolations of nostalgia. The Old Right not only lacked a program. It could not explain, even to itself, why and how the world had changed.

But someone else could. James Burnham was one of a small breed of ex-Communist intellectuals appalled by Soviet crimes but still captive to the Marxist vision of history. Almost a caricature of the "Red decade" salon radical, Burnham, the son of a Chicago railroad executive, was educated at Princeton and Oxford, taught philosophy at New York University, and lived on Sutton Place, where his socially ambitious wife gave elegant dinner parties. Burnham, in formal dress, would excuse himself to read proofs of *The New International* delivered by messenger. But he was also a serious polemical thinker—in fact America's leading theorist of Trotskyism, collaborating with "the Old Man" himself to form the Socialist Workers Party. In 1937, when Trotsky had persisted in defending the Soviet Union even under the predations of his mortal enemy Stalin, Burnham began a quarrel that climaxed after the 1939 Nazi-Soviet pact. Trotsky tortuously endorsed it, while Burnham thought the pact exposed the true "exploitative and imperialist character of the Soviet regime." Trotsky denounced Burnham as an "educated witch-doctor" and "intellectual snob," and Burnham incinerated all his correspondence with the Old Man.

In 1940, Burnham started writing a book about "the rising tide of a world revolution" sweeping through Communist Russia, Nazi Germany, the nations of western Europe, and, to a lesser extent, the United States, obliterating surface differences among them. The world war might temporarily have made these nations combatants, but on a profounder level they were all moving in the same direction, "interlocked by myriad technological, economic, and cultural chains," though not by dictatorship, whether of the one-man or the one-party type. In fact, such terms had been drained of meaning. Power wasn't exerted by individual leaders, who were front men and figureheads, even if some, like Roosevelt, possessed "demagogic" gifts. The true vanguard of the global revolution was its submerged "elite," salaried mid-level managers, "the younger group of administrators, experts, technicians, bureaucrats," tucked invisibly in the substrata of "the state apparatus," greedily amassing secret power. The phenomenon was most apparent in Germany and the Soviet Union, with their rigidly organized hierarchies. But the United States was approaching a similar condition. Its ever-expanding bureaucracy had become a self-perpetuating, in-gathering system, increasingly centralized, ruled by apprentice radicals. By the time the young mandarins were finished, collec-tivism would have supplanted the ideal of the free market and private ownership.

The thesis was not wholly original, as Burnham freely ac-knowledged. Versions of it had been written long before by theo-rists like the sociologist Robert Michels, who had coined the expression "the iron law of oligarchy" to describe the tendency in all societies for power to accrue to an elite corps. Still, *The Mana-gerial Revolution* was an international sensation, not least because Burnham icily predicted an Axis victory in World War II—a scary but plausible outcome, given Germany's brutally efficient con-quest of France, the steady aerial punishment it was inflicting on London, and Germany's surprise invasion of Russia in the spring of 1941—an event that coincided with the book's publication. Burnham also envisioned a postwar global technocracy, domi-nated by a triad of "superstates," Japan, Germany, and the United States. (George Orwell, who read Burnham closely—and was al-ternately stimulated and appalled—would borrow this scheme for his novel *Nineteen Eighty-Four*.) Burnham's argument was in re-ality a parable about the naked pursuit of power. It was, he be-lieved, the only political story worth telling since all political schemes inescapably served the God of power. "No theory, no promises, no morality, no amount of good will, no religion will restrain power," he wrote. Even "great public documents such as constitutions, or declarations of independence or of the rights of man," were the instruments of domination, while ideologies of any kind, left or right, were analogous "to what is sometimes called 'rationalization' in the sphere of individual psychology," expediently deployed to advance "the social interests of the ruling class" and at the same time nourish "the sentiments of the masses."

Burnham's talents were essentially literary and journalistic. He had a flair for capturing the drama of advancing events. The very coolness of his prose heightened the suppressed melodrama of his argument. He organized the confusions and anxieties of the moment into a coherent explanation. His attack on the New Deal didn't seem an attack at all. It was too sophisticated, too detached, almost preening in its analytical punctilio. But in the end his conclusion did not differ from Herbert Hoover's. "No candid observer, friend or enemy of the New Deal," Burnham wrote, "can deny that in terms of economic, social, political, and ideological changes from traditional capitalism, the New Deal moves in the same direction as Stalinism and Nazism." Thus did Burnham originate the central argument of movement conservatism. Soon he would be joined by others, ex-Trotskyists and ex-Stalinists who moved to the right but remained in some sense captive to the Left. Persuaded they were living in revolutionary times, they retained their absolutist fervor, replacing the Marxist dialectic with a Manichaean politics of good and evil, still with us today.

The complication was that Rooseveltism worked. By 1945, when the war ended, the United States had established itself as the world's dominant superpower. In 1948, Roosevelt's successor, Harry Truman, was elected president, the Democrats' fifth consecutive victory, dating back to 1932. The sun had enlarged to colossal proportions. Not only the Right was worried. "We shall have a first class fascist party in the United States if the Republicans don't win," the columnist Joseph Alsop, Beltway sage and Georgetown Brahmin, wrote in the *New York Herald Tribune*. "The real need for a change in this country arises, not from the decay of the Democrats, but from the need to give the Republicans the sobering experience of responsibility," lest they degenerate into a fringe opposition.

Others put it more clinically. "To solidify itself permanently in American life the New Deal needs at least one Republican victory," Samuel Lubell wrote in *The Future of American Politics*, published in time for the election. "Once in office the Republicans will automatically endorse much of the New Deal, through the simple device of leaving things untouched." Not even the most ardent hater of government was about to scale back a federal civilian workforce that had quadrupled (from 630,000 to 2.5 million) since the GOP had last been in power or slash a budget that had multiplied by twenty-two (from $3.8 billion to $85.4 billon). What politician, save one bent on self-destruction, would try to revoke Social Security or undo subsidies the public had grown to expect? As Lubell put it: "Extreme right-wing Republicans, who talk as if they would repeal every law passed in the last twenty years, would find they had to accept much of the New Deal under Republican administrators."

But the candidate of the party faithful, Senator Robert A. Taft, had different ideas. The leader of the conservative coalition that had blocked so many of Roosevelt's initiatives in his second term, Taft pledged to roll back the New Deal. Denied the nomination repeatedly since 1940, he now was plainly owed it. But GOP chieftains, East Coast moderates led by Thomas Dewey, the twice-defeated nominee, in 1944 and 1948, favored Dwight Eisenhower, the hero of World War II. Eisenhower was not a committed conservative. He had served loyally under Truman and was, moreover, a protégé of Truman's first secretary of state, George Marshall, who had "lost" China to the Communists. But Eisenhower could win, and Taft could not. Or so the Republican leadership believed. If the "moon" party was to avoid a sixth consecutive defeat, Eisenhower was the answer. The disagreement was not only strategic. It was also regional (the East Coast versus the heartland) and temperamental (realism versus revanchism). And it resulted in "one of the great party struggles in American history," as the New Yorker's political correspondent Richard Rovere wrote at the time. The convention, in Chicago, was a scene of intense conflict—complete with charges of delegate stealing. Eisenhower won, in a display of power by Dewey's wing, "the same old gang of Eastern Internationalists and Republican New Dealers who ganged up to sell the Republican Party down the river in 1940, in 1944, and in 1948," as a convention broadside put it. One Taft delegate, exiting the Hilton hotel after Eisenhower's anointment, grimly declared, "This means eight more years of socialism."

There were elaborate gestures of conciliation. Taft, toting a briefcase with a small-government manifesto inside, paid a call on "the General" in his Manhattan apartment, and emerged as triumphant as Grant at Appomattox. But that was in September, an eternity before Election Day. It left Eisenhower ample time to burnish his moderate credentials. He delivered a smashing victory in November, but to the Right it just confirmed that any

Republican could have won, including the "unelectable" Taft, who might well have outdone "Eisenhewey" in getting Republican legislators elected. Eisenhower had been victorious as Ike—the beloved "soldier of democracy"—not as the leader of his party. For all his vaunted coattails, Republicans held only the slimmest of advantages in Congress, a mere seven votes in the House while the Senate was tied, though Vice President Nixon could break the deadlock as needed.

Thus, while Olympian outsiders, the Alsops and Walter Lippmanns, apostles of consensus and bipartisanship, of "responsible" leadership, settled into the new era of Aquarian calm, others sensed an impending revolt that might crack the Republican Party wide open. And if Taft, who declared himself willing to work with the new administration, declined to mobilize "the rebel elements," they would mobilize themselves.

And everyone knew who they were. Throughout the Roosevelt-Truman years the source of conservative power had been Congress, particularly after 1938, when the Democrats had been punished in congressional elections. They were still in the majority, but the Republicans gained seventy seats. The public was wearying of endless New Dealism, and many were alienated by Roosevelt's Court-packing scheme. It was in 1938 that the House Committee on Un-American Activities (HUAC) came into existence. Its first chairman, Martin Dies, a Texas Democrat, denounced the New Deal's infiltration by "idealists, dreamers, politicians, professional 'do-gooders,' and just plain job hunters."

The last category was the most illuminating. Those who sought government jobs were automatically suspect. With the advent of the Cold War, the investigations changed in character. The job hunters—more precisely, the faceless managerial elite—might in fact be secret Communists. Conservative House Republicans leaped on the issue, helping unmask the onetime Soviet agent Alger Hiss in 1948. After Hiss's perjury conviction, the Red investigations shifted to the Senate, thanks to Joseph McCarthy, who, with encouragement from Taft, began a clamorous campaign to expose subversives concealed in the upper reaches of the "state apparatus."

McCarthy hadn't read Burnham. He didn't need to. He operated on instincts perfectly pitched to the anxious Cold War moment. Stalin was tightening his grip on Central and Eastern Europe, the site of show trials and purges. China fell to the Communists. Who was to blame? McCarthy knew—or pretended to. The culprits were enemies within, those blessed with "the finest homes, the finest education and the finest jobs in government."

McCarthy gave the Right something it had been missing for generations, authentic populist fervor. The cerebral, remote Taft lacked it. But not "Tailgunner Joe." The legend still persists that his targets were "little people," dissenters, immigrants, freethinkers, "Fifth Amendment Communists." And these were in fact among his incidental victims—the occasional journalist or "Red-ucator" summoned for a grilling. But McCarthy's true accomplishment, if that's the word, was to refresh the Right's long-running war on "Washington bureaucrats" and "big government." And he led the incursion into the citadels of American power—the State Department, the CIA, and eventually the Army and the White House. He was the conservatives' first insurrectionist. His cry of "twenty years of treason" drew on the banked passions of the Right, America First isolationists, small-business men, Catholic organizations. Patrick J. Buchanan, an adolescent during McCarthy's peak years, would later praise him (in his memoir *Right from the Beginning*) for doing "to the American Establishment precisely what the New Deal Democrats had done to corporate America and Wall Street. He shattered, forever, the nation's confidence in their capacity to govern." The notion of government itself as the "enemy" of the Republic is a familiar one in our history. But McCarthy was the author of what would become a staple of GOP politics over the next half century: the raid on government mounted from within government itself. Later practitioners included Richard Nixon (Watergate), Ronald Reagan (Iran-contra), Newt Gingrich (twice: the government shutdown of 1995 and then Bill Clinton's impeachment), and George W. Bush (his dismissals of nine U.S. attorneys). Like McCarthy's crusade, these later insurgencies were conceived in a spirit of hatred for a liberal elite who were perceived to be usurpers and hence subversives. For McCarthy's followers the New Deal, with its mildly radical reforms administered by Ivy League graduates, was tantamount to treason. In 1950, after Dean Acheson, Marshall's successor as secretary of state, had voiced sympathy for the convicted Hiss, his underling some years before, the Nebraska senator Hugh Butler was beside himself: "I look at that fellow, I watch his smart-aleck manner and his British clothes and that New Dealism in everything he says and does, and I want to shout, 'Get out! Get out! You stand for everything that has been wrong in the United States for years!'" This was the essence of McCarthyism, of what Buchanan called its "boisterous, bellowing call for the overthrow of [America's] reigning Establishment."

The protest was registered simultaneously on another front, by one of McCarthy's most exuberant intellectual champions,

William F. Buckley Jr., whose first book, *God and Man at Yale*, had excited a furious controversy when it was published in 1951. Buckley accused his alma mater of having fostered "one of the most extraordinary incongruities of our time: the institution that derives its moral and financial support from Christian individualists and then addresses itself to the task of persuading the sons of those supporters to be atheistic socialists."

On the surface, this argument seemed fatally narrow. Who cared what opinions Yale professors held or what textbooks they assigned? But Buckley, at age twenty-five, wrote with the full-throated passion of the agitator, his slashing debater's style borrowed, it seemed, from Red-hunting inquisitions: the naming of names, the quick, mocking characterizations, the trotting out of ideological résumés. It all added up to a breathless news report, a kind of "Ivy League Confidential," its true subject the revolution that had occurred at the Olympian reaches of American society, its true message that the political program of the last generation, New Deal liberalism, had been enshrined as intellectual and cultural dogma.

"The conservatives, as a minority, are the new radicals," Buckley wrote, and it was indeed his book's radicalism that set it apart. When Buckley described "the power of the machine and techniques that are so readily available to the academic 'liberals' for immediate use against anyone meddlesome enough to find fault with existing policy," he prefigured the next decade's campus radicals, leftists who likewise inveighed against the "machine" of large universities and their power to crush dissent. It was difficult, in any case, to refute Buckley's assertion that Yale professors, however liberal their politics might be, cultivated their own orthodoxy. They were the academic equivalents of the

Washington mandarins who contrived the fiction of "consensus"—the "nonpartisan" foreign policy that muted all debate, the polite "Ivy League anti-Communism" that silenced Joe McCarthy, the tepid stage-managed presidential election that limited the choices to the bland Ike and the staid Adlai Stevenson.

To his intellectual champions, McCarthy the man mattered less than McCarthy*ism*, "a movement around which men of good will and stern morality can close ranks," Buckley declared in his second book, *McCarthy and His Enemies*, written in collaboration with his brother-in-law and Yale classmate, L. Brent Bozell, with much of the material drawn from McCarthy's own files. The authors argued that McCarthyism was actually the expression of the higher "conformity" all ordered societies invoked to deter internal subversion. Just as sentient people might "speak of the 'conformity' of English sentiment on, say, the subject of parliamentary government," so they should embrace McCarthyism, "an orthodoxy-in-the-making."

This argument was furnished by Willmoore Kendall, who had taught the co-authors at Yale and was the de facto editor of *God and Man at Yale* and now of this second book. In Kendall's theory, McCarthy was the tribune of America's defining politics of majoritarianism. His thunderous attacks on Communism reflected his intuitive grasp that "domestic communism" was a threat to the civil order. The secondary danger came from liberals who contributed to the problem by recasting the issue in terms of constitutional rights and the rule of law, even as Communists and fellow travelers cleverly exploited those same protections. The liberals, thoroughly taken in, didn't get what the man on the street felt in his bones, that Communism was the unassimilable Other and must be expunged by whatever means worked. If not, democracy itself was in danger. "Some day," wrote Buckley and Bozell, "the patience of America may at last be exhausted, and we will strike out against Liberals. Not because they are treacherous like Communists, but because, with James Burnham, we will conclude 'that they are mistaken in their predictions, false in their analyses, wrong in their advice, and through the results of their actions injurious to the nation.' "

Published in the spring of 1954, in time for the televised spectacle of the Army-McCarthy hearings, *McCarthy and His Enemies* made the *Times*'s best-seller list, even as McCarthy self-destructed in full public view. Buckley, invited to address a pro-McCarthy rally in midtown Manhattan, told a crowd of more than two thousand—with the spillover massed in the street or thronging benches in Bryant Park—that McCarthy was the heir of "the abolitionists of a hundred years ago" and like them a victim of moral cowardice, particularly among the press, with its "cynical attitude of malice toward a man who has put his finger on something that should have been exposed by the press itself."

McCarthy's rise and fall, for all its swiftness, completed the movement's adoption of insurgency as a style of politics. Together, Buckley and McCarthy grasped that the ground of political conflict had shifted. The war of ideology was also a war of class. Others saw this, too. In his essay "The Pseudo-Conservative Revolt," published in 1954, Richard Hofstadter theorized that McCarthyism represented a new "dynamic of dissent" best understood as a form of cultural protest, evidence that politics itself was assuming a new character. "The growth of the mass media of communication and their use in politics have brought politics closer to the people than ever before and have made politics a form of entertainment in which the spectators feel themselves involved. Thus it has become, more than ever before, an arena into which private emotions and personal problems can be readily projected. Mass communications have made it possible to keep the mass man in an almost constant state of political mobilization."

"Who rules this country?" Buckley asked in the summer of 1954. "Certainly not 'business' (as the leftists claim). The nearest thing we have to a 'ruling class' in America is the 'opinion makers'—newspapermen, publishers, commentators, educators, ministers and members of the various professions."

These were the opening sentences of the "selling memo" Buckley drafted for a new magazine he hoped to edit, one that might "correct the sorry situation of today where the liberal appears to have a monopoly on sophisticated information." This document, in its raw state, effectively laid out the movement's line of attack over the next half century, as did Buckley's insistence, in correspondence with potential backers, that conservatives must resist the temptation "to realign conservative principles to harmonize" with Eisenhower's modified New Dealism, so sharp a descent from the Republicanism of 1928, the year of Hoover's election. The enemy was, once again, the man in the White House, only now he was a Republican, complicit in "a slow drift toward neutralism, continued welfarism, and softness toward labor unions and the bureaucracy."

Conservatives were losing the big battles not because their positions failed to resonate with the country at large, Buckley was sure, but because "there was no audible, resourceful public voice" to counter "the manipulated argument of the left," which fixed the conditions of debate and thus controlled its outcome.

Thus was born *National Review*. Its early brain trust included

Burnham and Kendall. But the figure Buckley was keenest to re-
cruit was Whittaker Chambers, America's most famous repen-
tant ex-Communist—a onetime Soviet spy whose testimony
against his confederate Alger Hiss had given the movement its
animating cause. In the mid-1950s, Chambers's moral authority
exceeded that of any other conservative intellectual, the conse-
quence of his testimony, first before HUAC and then in the courtroom. He was superbly cast in the role of witness-accuser, with
his gravid air of fatalism, of persecution and guilt, of tormented
secrecy and penitential disclosure. Chambers had paid a heavy
price for his testimony. He had lost a good job at *Time* magazine
and been banished from the charmed circle of American intellectuals. He had then written his memoir, *Witness*, which distilled
the superpower conflict in its starkest Manichaean terms as a war
between "two irreconcilable faiths . . . Communism and Freedom . . . All the politics of our time, including the politics of war,
will be the politics of this crisis."

Chambers was now living in self-imposed exile on his Maryland farm. Buckley visited him there in 1954 and over the next
several months pleaded with him to join forces with *National Review*. But Chambers turned him down for various reasons. For
one, he had dealt with McCarthy and was convinced he was a
"raven of disaster" who would cause conservatives more trouble than he was worth. For another, the trauma of the Hiss case
behind him, Chambers had moved past his counterrevolution-
ary phase and now embraced a genuinely classical conservatism. He distilled his thinking in a remarkable sequence of
letters written to Buckley from 1954 till Chambers's death in
1961. Published (in 1969) as *Odyssey of a Friend*, they constitute
one of the great documents of modern conservatism, a flowing

private narrative of observations, reminiscences, *pensées,* and tutorials written by a scarred survivor of the century's ideological catastrophes.

Chambers sympathized with *National Review*'s theoretical opposition to increasingly centralized government. But, in practical terms, he believed challenging it was futile, at least on the terms the Right was pursuing. The movement might potentially have "all the brains, money and other resources it needs. But it can never mobilize them because it lacks one indispensable: it has no program . . . [and] for one reason: it will not face historical reality."

That reality was obvious: the regulatory economics of the New Deal had become the basis for governing in postwar America, and conservatives had no plausible choice but to accept this fact—not because liberals were all-powerful but because what the Right depicted as "statist" meddling by an overweening government looked instead like a needed Burkean "correction."

Chambers knew this because he saw fresh evidence of it every day. He raised milch cattle, and his neighbors were farmers. Most were archconservative, even reactionary. They had sent the segregationist Democrat Millard Tydings to the Senate, and then, when Tydings had opposed McCarthy's Red-hunting investigations, they had voted him out of office. They were also sworn enemies of programs like FDR's Agricultural Adjustment Act (Hiss had been on its staff in its first days), which tried to offset the volatility of markets by controlling crop yields and fixing prices. The programs had then been adjusted for wartime, first during World War II and then again during the Korean War. Eisenhower's Labor Department had perpetuated this policy, greatly increasing the sums directed toward stabilizing farm income. With this came further irksome restrictions. Some of Chambers's neighbors had been indicted for refusing to allow farm officials to inspect their crops. Yet these same conservative farmers happily accepted federal subsidies. In other words, they wanted it both ways. They wanted the freedom to grow as much as they could, even though it was against their best interests. But they also expected the government to bail them out in difficult times. In sum, Chambers told Buckley, "the farmers are signing for a socialist agriculture with their feet."

And with good reason. To Chambers, an avid student of history, well schooled in Marxist argument, it was obvious that the growing dependency on government was a function of the unstoppable rise of industrial capitalism and the new technology it had brought forth. "The machine has made the economy socialistic," he wrote. And the Right had better adjust. "A conservatism that will not accept this situation . . . is not a political force, or even a twitch: it has become a literary whimsy." It might well be "the duty of the intellectuals . . . to preach reaction," but only "from an absolute, an ideal standpoint. It is for books and posterity. It does not bear on tactics or daily life . . . Those who remain in the world, if they will not surrender on its terms, must maneuver within its terms. That is what conservatives must decide: how much to give in order to survive at all; how much to give in order not to give up the basic principles."

It sounded like Burke, though Chambers occupied what he called "the Beaconsfield position," meaning the Earl of Beaconsfield—that is, Benjamin Disraeli. He was, after Burke, the second great figure in classical conservatism and its preeminent statesman. In his long career, which spanned most of the nineteenth century, Disraeli advocated "just, necessary, expedient" policies—

that is, the policies the public demanded even though they might contradict the conservative leader's own ideological certitudes. Disraeli conceived this approach during the Industrial Revolution, when a rising class of capitalists began to accumulate vast wealth and demanded more say in a government still dominated by the Crown and landed aristocrats, with even the right of suffrage limited to a small fraction of the (male) population. At first, Disraeli favored the status quo. The monarchy, he believed, bound different classes together, and centuries of feudal obligation had instilled in the nobility a deep sense of responsibility to the poor, so many of whom were vulnerable to exploitation in the industrialists' factories and workhouses. But ultimately, Disraeli realized the futility of this argument. As a statesman, he became an innovative reformer, partly to outflank the Liberals, partly to keep the Conservative Party viable in a time of dynamic upheaval, but also because he came to see that in the modern age, conservatism must stand for a benevolent, inclusive government that guarded the interests, needs, and rights of the entire population.

Chambers was not alone in seeing a divide between classical conservative thought and the polarizing politics of the movement. Indeed he seems to have been influenced by Arthur Schlesinger Jr.'s essay "The Politics of Nostalgia," published in June 1955, five months before the first issue of *National Review* appeared. Schlesinger's subject was the unexpected rise of "conservatism as a respectable social philosophy" in the postwar period. One book in particular, Russell Kirk's *The Conservative Mind,* a sumptuously written survey of the classical Anglo-American tradition of the eighteenth and nineteenth centuries, had attracted much attention. But Schlesinger noted a strange disconnect. Kirk and other "New Conservatives" genuinely revered traditional conservatism. And yet once "they leave the stately field of rhetoric and get down to actual issues of social policy, they tend quietly to forget about Burke and Disraeli and to adopt the views of the American business community." Kirk, for example, sounded like a plutocrat when he denounced federally sponsored school lunch programs as a "vehicle for totalitarianism" and Social Security as a form of "remorseless collectivism."

Where in this, Schlesinger asked, was even a hint of classical conservatism, with its sober accounting of the social and moral costs of unchecked industrial capitalism? "Disraeli with his legislation on behalf of trade unions, his demand for government intervention to improve working conditions, his belief in due process and civil freedom, his support for the extension of the suffrage, his insistence on the principle of compulsory education! If there is anything in contemporary America that might win the instant sympathy of men like [Lord] Shaftesbury and Disraeli, it could well be the school-lunch program. But for all his talk about mutual responsibility and the organic character of society, Professor Kirk, when he gets down to cases, tends to become a roaring Manchester liberal of the Herbert Hoover school."

This wasn't quite fair. Schlesinger rather conveniently emphasized Kirk's retrograde pronouncements when another "New Conservative," Peter Viereck, had supported Adlai Stevenson in 1952 and had accused McCarthy of "subverting precisely those institutions that are the most conservative and organic, everything venerable and patrician, from the Constitution, and precisely the most decorated or paternal generals . . . to the leaders of our most deeply established religion and precisely the most ancient of our universities."

For years to come the Right would remain split between the Burkean-Disraelian politics adjustment, whose centrist thinkers and politicians devoutly supported the existing political order, and the revanchist politics of counterrevolution, which sought to bring that order down. At *National Review* the revanchists dominated. Some talked of a third-party movement, sheer "crackpotism," in Chambers's view. "I am . . . so firmly opposed to a third party," he told Buckley, "that I cannot permit my name to be used in any way that might imply that I support or abet it or anything connected with it."

In 1956, Burnham alone among *NR* editors endorsed Eisenhower's reelection, pointing out that political parties in America were not "ideological or class organizations." Another ex-Trotskyist, William Schlamm, an infatuated McCarthyite, urged conservatives to sit out the election, while Buckley joined a far-right contingent keen to mount a third-party challenge. Garry Wills, who joined the staff of *National Review* in 1957, was struck by the editors' "deliberately rootless kind of conservatism, one that would have no truck with liberals . . . It, for the first time, made Liberalism (capitalized) the Enemy . . . Buckley knew Liberalism only as an object of attack. In line with this offensive policy, Buckley gave the magazine a predominantly monitoring task. It came to accuse," extending the line of battle Buckley had drawn in his books on Yale and McCarthy. Wills, for his part, urged a consensus conservatism that "can give the practical art of politics a combination of flexibility and stability" and also "seek 'the common good,' not as some ideal scheme of order, or quantitative accumulation of individual goods, but as the real life of the 'commonality,' of community in all its enriching forms."

Chambers, agreeing at last to write for *National Review* in 1957, clung to the Beaconsfield position. He supported the Eisenhower administration's negotiations with the Soviets and surprised readers with his defense of civil liberties, including Hiss's right to the passport the State Department issued him in 1959: "To me, travel restriction seems chiefly to multiply the files behind which bureaucracies always gratefully barricade and entrench their positions, and fiercely defend them . . . A little shift in the political weather, and it may be the spokesmen of the Right whose freedom of travel is restricted." He also praised John Kenneth Galbraith's "witty and bracingly arrogant" critique of "the affluent society," which had shirked its obligations toward the disadvantaged. "One of the beneficent side-effects of the crisis of the twentieth century as a whole," Chambers wrote, "is a dawning realization, not so much that the mass of mankind is degradingly poor, as that there will be no peace for the islands of relative plenty until the continents of proliferating poverty have been lifted to something like the general material level of the islanders."

Chambers's most important contribution to the magazine was an elegant dismantling of Ayn Rand's *Atlas Shrugged*, with its avid pursuit of individual material gain, its rigid claims of certitude, its intolerance of dissent. "At first, we try to tell ourselves that these are just lapses, that this mind has, somehow, mislaid the discriminating knack that most of us pray will warn us in time of the difference between what is effective and firm, and what is wildly grotesque and excessive," Chambers wrote. "Soon we suspect something worse. We suspect that this mind finds, precisely in extravagance, some exalting merit; feels a surging release of power and passion precisely in smashing up the house." This was a critique not just of Rand but of all movement orthodoxy.

At first these debates were intellectual sideshows, with no overt connection to the actual politics of the time. The 1950s were the apex of bipartisan consensus—"the strong, confident, center-of-the-road American Consensus," as Arthur Larson, Eisenhower's undersecretary of labor, wrote in his book *A Republican Looks at His Party,* published in 1956. The twin engines of what Eisenhower called the "military-industrial complex" and the booming postindustrial economy fostered the interdependence of government and business and appeared to have erased the divide between left and right.

The issue was competence. In the 1958 elections, held amid a crippling recession, Democrats scored a massive victory in congressional and statewide races. In the survey *The American Voter,* published in 1960, researchers at the University of Michigan reported that only one-fourth of the electorate held fixed, or even clear, opinions on most issues or identified those positions with one party or the other. A mere 2 percent could be classified as holding a consistently "ideological" position on overall policy. These results were not really startling. But they put movement thinkers in a curious position. To maintain that the "elite" alone was responsible for liberal election triumphs was to verge, if not on "crackpotism," then at least on conspiracism.

In an influential book, *The End of Ideology*, published in 1960, the sociologist Daniel Bell described a post-cataclysmic world, exhausted by totalitarian dogmas, with Americans in particular "resistant to the old terms of ideological debate between 'left' and 'right.' " This theme was picked up by the Kennedy administration in its embrace of technology-driven pragmatism. Even more than Eisenhower, Kennedy operated outside or "beyond" ideology. At a press conference in 1962, he asserted that while "most of us are conditioned for many years to have a political viewpoint—Republican or Democratic, liberal, conservative or moderate," in fact the most pressing problems of the day are "technical problems, administrative problems" that "do not lend themselves to the great sort of passionate movements which have stirred this country so often in the past." While the Right remained locked in orthodoxy, the nation was meeting on the common ground of consensus.

Only right-wing eggheads seemed to be missing the drift. "To William F. Buckley, Jr., and his collaborators on the *National Review*," Richard Rovere wrote in "The American Establishment," an essay lampooning the growing fixation on the power elite, the "Establishment includes just about everyone in the country except themselves and the great hidden, enlightened majority of voters who would, if only they were given the chance, put a non-Establishment man in the White House and have [Kennedy's ambassador] John Kenneth Galbraith recalled from India or left there and relieved of his passport."

This was the mirthful view from the ramparts of consensus liberalism. But conservatives sensed something else, an ideological vacuum. None did so more clearly than Brent Bozell, who had written speeches for Joe McCarthy and then Goldwater and was himself a casualty of the 1958 Democratic sweep, when he campaigned for a seat in the Maryland House of Delegates. He lost, but the experience of meeting voters face-to-face taught Bozell what every working politician knew and the Michigan survey confirmed: most voters were neither on the left nor on the right but instead were crowded in a "vast uncommitted middle" and, "though today they vote for Democratic or Modern Republican candidates, are not ideologically wedded to their programs or, for that matter, to any program." The country, perhaps, was not so much *post-* as *pre-*ideological. The passions and grievances of the past hadn't disappeared—and never would, not even in a relatively contented time. They remained present, if invisible, below the placid surface, and could be touched and stirred. There were, potentially, new constituents for the Right. "The problem is to reach out and organize them."

Actually, some were being organized, through the auspices of the John Birch Society, established in 1958, the year after Mc-Carthy's death. Today the organization is best remembered for the inventive theorizing of its founder, Robert Welch, who unearthed arcane evidence of Soviet influence in almost every zone of American life. But what Welch, a retired businessman, lacked in analytical acumen he made up for in organizational brio. His inspiration was to create a virtually counter-Communist conspiracy, whose members dutifully mailed in monthly slices of their annual dues ($24 for men, $21 for women) and received in turn a monthly bulletin calling their attention to the latest incursion of the Red menace. Welch claimed to command a total network numbering 100,000 and predicted it would reach 1 million by 1963. What was more, Birchers were often upstanding members of the community who joined the organization as they had joined the Chamber of Commerce or the Elks Club—and the Republican Party. One could be a Bircher and still maintain one's normal political affiliations. At the organization's first meeting in Indianapolis, Welch handed copies of his book *The Politician* to the eleven men in attendance, who read assertions like this: "In my opinion, the chances are very strong that Milton Eisenhower is actually Dwight Eisenhower's superior and boss within the Communist Party." The eleven "were rich men, most of them first-generation rich, all determined to protect what they had acquired for themselves in the free-enterprise way," *Look* magazine reported in 1961. "They read *The Politician*, and they told Welch it would not do." It soon disappeared from circulation. And since Welch had printed it himself, it wasn't registered with the Library of Congress (it is today).

All this fed the Birchers' mystique. When they set up a "pilot" program in Wichita, Kansas, business kings joined. Visiting the campus of Wichita University, Welch told an audience of two thousand about Communist infiltration of the Protestant ministry, and about research foundations laboring "to change the economic and political structure of the United States [so] that it can be comfortably merged with Soviet Russia."

Another stronghold was the Southwest, home to so many of the "wealthy businessmen, retired military officers and little old ladies in tennis shoes" who were seeking companionship among the lonely crowds in Orange County's exfoliating suburbs, where the tentacles of "the military-industrial complex" were spreading ever farther along the sunstruck frontier. Squeezed in between ocean and desert, a new class of middle managers at defense-related companies like Hughes Aircraft and Ford Aeronutronic—existing in parallel to the managerial elite Burnham had described—prospered alongside real estate speculators and "ranchers-turned-property-developers," not to mention "housewives, doctors, dentists, engineers," Lisa Mc-Girr writes in *Suburban Warriors*, her closely researched monograph on the emergence of Orange County as a hive of Birch activism in the 1960s. These supposed exemplars of the "paranoid style," nursing "luxurious hostilities" (the phrases are Richard Hofstadter's), actually "enjoyed the fruits of consumer culture, reveled in their worldly success, and, for the most part, found the suburban world of tract homes, private developments, and decentralized living to their liking," McGirr notes. "At living-room bridge clubs, at backyard barbecues, and at kitchen coffee klatches, the middle-class men and women of Orange County 'awakened' to what they perceived as the threats of communism and liberalism."

By this time, movement intellectuals realized the path to power ran through, not against, the GOP, especially once they found a tribune, Barry Goldwater, who stood as far to the right as they did. Goldwater's book *The Conscience of a Conservative*, ghostwritten by Brent Bozell, and the most influential political manifesto of the postwar period, promised a total dismantling of the welfare state. "I have little interest in streamlining government or in making it more efficient, for I mean to reduce its size," Goldwater/Bozell wrote. "I do not undertake to promote welfare, for I propose to extend freedom. My aim is not to pass laws, but to repeal them. It is not to inaugurate new programs, but to cancel old ones that do violence to the Constitution, or that have failed in their purpose, or that impose on the people an unwarranted financial burden."

In the spring of 1960 a second grassroots organization, Young Americans for Freedom (YAF), was formed on Buckley's family estate in Sharon, Connecticut, where ninety or so young conservatives gathered to compose a revanchist manifesto that concisely listed twelve "certain eternal truths," among them that "the market economy . . . is the single economic system compatible with the requirements of personal freedom and constitutional government" and "the forces of international Communism are, at present, the greatest single threat to these liberties," which necessitated, in turn, "that the United States should stress victory over, rather than coexistence with, this menace."

In March 1962, YAF staged a rally at Madison Square Garden, with some eighteen thousand in attendance. The guest of honor was Goldwater. Bozell, himself only thirty-six and an orator of re-markable skills—at Yale he had often outshone Buckley when the pair had been debate partners—thundered forth the movement's demands: "To the Joint Chiefs of Staff: Make the necessary prepa-rations for a landing in Havana . . . To our commander in Berlin: Tear down the Wall . . . To the chief of C.I.A.: You are under in-structions to encourage liberation movements in every nation of the world under Communist domination, including the Soviet Union itself." The event received front-page coverage in *The New York Times*. Soon after, the paper published a four-part report on the new phenomenon of campus political movements, left and right.

That summer a very different group of young activists convened in Michigan to form a new leftist organization, Students for a Democratic Society (SDS). It, too, produced a document, the Port Huron Statement, principally written by the group's charismatic leader, Tom Hayden. The contrast between the two student documents captures the crucial distinction between the New Right and the New Left. Not one of the items in the Sharon Statement would have unsettled Herbert Hoover or Robert A. Taft. It was a reassertion of movement faith. The Port Huron Statement, a much longer document, radiated generational protest. Repudiating "the liberal and socialist preachments of the past," Hayden emphasized moral and spiritual "values." He called for "power and uniqueness rooted in love, reflectiveness, reason, and creativity" and a "political order" that would "provide outlets for the expression of personal grievance and aspiration." It might have been written by a politicized Holden Caulfield.

The rise of these two competing movements was noted by elders, and some were alarmed. Writing in *The New York Times Magazine*, the Democratic congressman John Brademas (later the president of New York University) observed that "the intensity of student interest in politics has increased on both ends of the political scale, Left and Right," and that "the most militant, self-proclaimed conservatives or liberals tend to move to extreme positions." The danger, Brademas warned, was that both camps seemed to be repudiating "our two major political parties."

Brademas got it half-right. Many on the New Left would indeed go on to reject traditional elective politics and declare their own war against "the establishment." Some SDS factions took up violence. But the young radicals of the Right, thanks in part to Buckley and Bozell, stayed within the orbit of conventional politics. They helped organize Goldwater's first blunted stab at the Republican presidential nomination in 1960 and later served as foot soldiers, and in some cases leaders, in the "Draft Goldwater" movement that catalyzed the next election. YAF "added 5,400 recruits in the summer of 1964, compared to SDS's total membership of 1,500," Rick Perlstein notes in *Before the Storm*, his account of the Goldwater campaign.

The Birchers played a major part, too. "The epicenter of Southern California conservatism—Orange County—took the lead in mobilizing the groundswell for Goldwater," McGirr writes. "In 1964 the region from Fullerton to Laguna Beach, Yorba Linda to Irvine was Goldwater country." His vote totals there were surpassed only in the Deep South. A year later, there were some ten thousand Birchers in the state, and five thousand in Orange County alone.

Goldwater went down to catastrophic defeat, and many assumed, or hoped, that the movement's "death sentence was firmly spoken," Buckley observed in a fund-raising letter to *National Review* subscribers, who now numbered 100,000. In fact, Goldwater's loss "was not a great defeat, but rather a great disappointment," Buckley wrote. The chances of a victory had always been slim, since Kennedy's assassination all but guaranteed the election of his successor, Lyndon Johnson. And the landslide, great though it was, did not erase Goldwater's twenty-seven million votes.

But the most important lesson was generational. Goldwater's vast army of volunteers reached 3.9 million, according to Perlstein, twice as many as worked for Johnson. The establishment Republicans who fought to deny him the nomination—William Scranton, George Romney, Henry Cabot Lodge, Nelson Rockefeller, all illustrious names in 1964—ended up marginalized within the party. Most have faded from public memory. But the Goldwaterite Robert Bork would play an important role in the Nixon and the Reagan years. And in 2000, the Goldwaterite William Rehnquist would hoist George W. Bush into the presidency. The Goldwater legacy endured for many years to come.

The comparison with Kennedy is instructive. The Kennedy myth, reinforced by his martyrdom, was that he was a Pied Piper who captivated American youth through idealistic programs like the Peace Corps and with his call to break with the 1950s and its complacent quietism. But as Garry Wills pointed out in *Nixon Agonistes: The Crisis of the Self-Made Man,* his classic account of 1960s politics, "the incontrovertible point of campus revolt [was that] it came about *under Kennedy,* during a liberal regime, when youth was hopeful and the Establishment looked permeable by young ideas . . . the Bay of Pigs had occurred . . . SDS and SNCC were founded, the Port Huron Statement was adopted—all these things happened *before* Kennedy's death." Kennedy, in other words, had loosed generational forces but could not contain them. The next wave of liberals became, in many cases, leftists swept by the tide of protest away from the established centers of power, and away from government itself.

But the opposite happened on the right. The one unassailable contribution of movement conservatism, and it is an important one, is that its passions were channeled into the normative institutions of electoral politics—its parties, its campaigns, its candidates. The movement can be accused of much, but its legions seldom took to the streets. Rather than trying to overthrow the established political order, its followers sought to wrest control of it even as they waged war against the "liberal establishment."

To his followers, especially the youngest of them, Goldwater had the virtue of seeming to violate the strictures of consensus. He "attacked not only liberals and Democrats, but Republicans as well," John A. Andrew III writes in *The Other Side of the Sixties: Young Americans for Freedom and the Rise of Conservative Politics.* "This gave his message an aura of principled purity that sharply contrasted with other rhetoric" in the 1960s.

At the time few noticed. The attention was on the period's civil and social disruptions. But even as the New Left degenerated into street theater and "happenings," New Right radicals continued to master the mechanics of the two-party system and to make it the vehicle of their insurgency.

3

———

TANGLED PATHOLOGIES

However exhilarating the Goldwater crusade had been, it did not immediately bring movement conservatives closer to power. On the contrary, it threatened to marginalize the Republican Party more drastically than at any time since the New Deal. In 1965, when Lyndon Johnson began his full term, Democrats occupied more than two-thirds of the seats in both the House and the Senate and held more than three-quarters of the nation's governorships. A mere 25 percent of the electorate identified itself as Republican. The moon had waned to near extinction.

And yet it was in this period that conservatism entered its greatest phase, a decade-long period, from 1965 to 1975, during which the familiar dynamic between orthodoxy and consensus underwent a remarkable reversal. The liberal sun, even as it steadily enlarged, swerved off its consensus course and strayed into the astral wastes of orthodoxy. And the conservative movement, building a coalition of disenchanted and alienated elements of the old Democratic coalition—blue-collar urban ethnics, Jewish and Catholic intellectuals repelled by the countercultural enthusiasms of the New Left—shaped a new consensus.

Like so many political transformations, it happened with startling swiftness. The first sign emerged only nine months after Johnson's massive victory. He had resumed office exuding confidence and ambition. Out from under Kennedy's shadow, he now was free to complete the unfinished business of the New Deal and graft onto the inherited programs of the New Frontier his own vision of a "Great Society." In a speech he gave at Howard University on June 4, 1965, Johnson introduced a sweeping new plan to cure the linked ills of racial discrimination and poverty. His opening words—"Our earth is the home of revolution"—were as dramatic as any uttered by a modern president. And those that followed were just as stirring, for Johnson took the rare step of speaking not of the country's successes but of its shortcomings, particularly in the area of race, this despite the recent triumphs of the civil rights movement, which Johnson vauntingly summarized. The Civil Rights Act of 1964—outlawing segregation in schools, public spaces, and the workplace—had been passed. Another major bill, the Voting Rights Act, would be signed shortly. These were historic measures. The country could be proud, especially African Americans, who had led the way—morally and politically. Showing "impressive restraint" in the struggle against Jim Crow, they had "peacefully protested and marched, entered the courtrooms and the seats of government, demanding a justice that has long been denied." This had secured them full citizenship and essential freedoms, "the right to share fully and equally in American society—to vote, to hold a job, to enter a public place, to go to school . . . to be treated in every part of our national life as a person equal in dignity and promise to all others."

But, Johnson went on to say, these gains, impressive though they were, could not obscure the "grimmer story" of "American failure." This was the dual story of economic and social injustice, which had become more grievous in a time of unrivaled national prosperity. In 1965 the gross national product grew 8 percent. Unemployment had sunk to 4.5 percent. And the federal budget office predicted a $45 billion growth in revenue over the next five years. For the majority of Americans the rewards were great. But the nation's twenty million blacks were falling ever further behind, particularly those trapped in cities, malign hatcheries of poverty and despair. An increasing number of black children were being raised in single-parent households, which in turn bred unemployment, delinquency, crime, and ultimately more poverty in what appeared to be an unbreakable cycle.

These conditions demanded more than legal redress, Johnson said. His administration hoped to cure the ills of inequality "through our poverty program, through our education program, through our medical care and our other health programs, and a dozen more of the Great Society programs." But even more was demanded. The struggle for black equality began with the irreducible first unit of civil society, the family. The legacy of slavery, with its brutally enforced separation of spouses and its sunderings of parents from children, had put blacks at a disadvantage they were still struggling to overcome. Johnson promised no immediate solutions but said they would emerge from a White House conference scheduled for the fall.

It was Johnson's most ringing speech, the most inspiring

by any president in recent memory. And its urgent message seemed perfectly timed. Racial protest had migrated out of the South and onto the more complex terrain of the North, where the issue was not the legalized injustices of Jim Crow but de facto discrimination in housing, education, and employment. This yielded a different form of racial protest. In the long, hot summer of 1964 a wave of rioting had swept through the urban Northeast—in Philadelphia, New York, Rochester. Unlike the southern disturbances, which had aroused sympathy in much of the nation, these new eruptions prompted an intense "white backlash," some of it registered in Democratic primaries, as the party of working-class solidarity fractured along racial lines. George Wallace, the arch-segregationist governor of Alabama, carried every white precinct in Gary, Indiana, and amassed heavy totals in Milwaukee's white ethnic wards.

Still, no one was prepared for what happened a summer later in Watts, a neighborhood in South Central Los Angeles where half a million blacks lived in placid and orderly, if overcrowded, conditions. In a comprehensive study published in 1964, the National Urban League, citing statistics "on housing, wages, income, delinquency, family life"—the same data the Johnson administration had been sifting through—concluded that blacks were better off in Watts than in any other urban zone in the country, thanks to California's governor, Pat Brown, and his administration, self-described "sons of the New Frontier and the Great Society," who had initiated an abundance of programs and services, from community centers to new schools to drug rehabilitation centers.

But in August, less than a week after Johnson signed the Voting Rights Act, Watts erupted in violence following a black teenager's arrest for drunken driving. For six days mobs rampaged, setting buildings ablaze amid an orgy of looting and vandalism. More than twelve thousand National Guardsmen were brought in. In the end, thirty-four people had been killed, more than a thousand injured, and nearly four thousand arrested.

Much of white America shuddered. The Reverend Billy Graham, the voice of Christian America, alarmed that racial unrest had gotten "out of hand," called for "salvation"—not from injustice, but from rioting. To others as well, the twenty million blacks for whom LBJ had vowed to fling open the gates now seemed "lawless brutes who have done nothing to deserve the good life in affluent America," Tom Wicker reported in *The New York Times.*

Conservatives at *National Review* had been expecting just such a rupture, partly because they viewed civil rights more skeptically—anachronistically, at times. The magazine had attacked the Supreme Court's desegregation ruling in 1954, siding with the upholders of Jim Crow, and had endorsed, in terms of strained gentility, the doctrine of racial superiority (though *National Review* had applauded the "economic sanctions" of the Montgomery bus boycott in 1955).

In any case, the Right saw a strategic opening. In 1963, *National Review*'s publisher, William Rusher, had urged Republicans, locked out of Dixie since the Civil War, to begin courting the votes of disaffected southern whites—the first outline of the "southern strategy" deployed by Goldwater in 1964 and Richard Nixon in 1968. Conservatives pursued this course guiltlessly. Whether or not racist themselves, they were not morally repulsed by racial prejudice, which to them was consonant with their preferred ideal of a hierarchical society. Even conservatives more sympathetic to civil rights detected an impending collision as the imperatives of racial justice clashed with the imperatives of civic order. In the early 1960s, Garry Wills, who sympathized with the demonstrators—and later became an impassioned admirer of Martin Luther King Jr.—argued that the "urgency" of black protest, and the natural inclination to satisfy it, might "bend the permanent structure of our society permanently out of shape" and so "sacrifice the peace of all of us to the demands (even legitimate demands) of some."

But it was Willmoore Kendall who analyzed the approaching crisis most rigorously. He was perhaps the only political thinker of the period, right or left, who viewed civil rights as a characteristic sociopolitical movement, in the tradition of abolitionism and suffrage. Like those other protests, Kendall wrote, the civil rights crusade dramatized two conflicting interpretations of the American tradition, each valid on its own terms. One was rooted in the radical-revolutionary vision of the Declaration of Independence, with its promise of full equality, further enshrined in the Gettysburg Address. Lincoln, the first modern liberal, had ushered in the age of "egalitarian reforms sanctioned by mandate emanating from national majorities." FDR and now LBJ had extended this tradition. Its latest iteration came in calls like those of Whitney M. Young Jr., the head of the National Urban League, for a race-based "Marshall Plan."

But there was a second tradition, of "conservative bias." It was recorded in *The Federalist Papers* and the Constitution. These creedal documents recorded the founders' resistance to the "demand for revolutionary changes in the American way of life" and their ideal of a Burkean modus vivendi that continually threw "obstacles in the path of those amongst us who have wished to use the power of government for effectuating major reshufflings of legal rights and duties and major shifts of powers from the state to the federal government." Full racial equality might be a laudable goal, but not one the government could create. It required a cultural transformation enacted on the micro level of "individuals, families, neighborhoods." And it could happen only over time through adaptations made gradually and "in a context of domestic tranquility."

Some liberals were having similar thoughts. Daniel Patrick Moynihan, an assistant secretary of labor first under Kennedy and then under Johnson, had helped formulate the war on poverty. His report "The Negro Family: The Case for National Action" was the source text for Johnson's speech at Howard (which Moynihan had co-written). But it also became a source of trouble.

Addressing a limited audience of decision makers, Moynihan, in blunt, urgent prose, described the chronic ills besetting inner-city blacks, above all the "drastic" increase in illegitimate births. Amid the enthusiasm that met the Howard speech, the report became public, and Moynihan was fiercely attacked—not by conservatives but, to his astonishment, by left-wing anti-poverty activists, who objected to his characterizations of blacks, especially to the phrase "tangle of pathology," though it was borrowed from Kenneth Clark, the distinguished African American social scientist. Moynihan, the author of a precedent-breaking proposal for aiding black families, found himself accused of "subtle racism" and labeled an "apologist for the white power structure." One hundred civil rights and religious leaders, gathering in New York, signed a resolution demanding "the question of 'family stability' be stricken" from the agenda of the scheduled White House conference.

"Before half-a-year had passed the initiative was in ruins, and after a year-and-a-half it is settled that nothing whatever came of it." So Moynihan wrote in 1967, in a retrospective essay that also assailed the Watts riot and its liberal defenders, some of whom depicted the rioters as "revolutionaries" or agents of protest. Moynihan's essay was published in *Commentary*, a monthly that, along with *The Public Interest*, was emerging as a venue for liberal writers and thinkers increasingly at odds with "the liberal Left," as Moynihan called it—radicals whose outlook seemed to mirror the anti-establishment passions of the Right. Like movement conservatives, these leftists ignored "the unpleasant facts of life for the poor—there is delinquency in the slums, but those kids in the suburbs are just as bad and don't get arrested, etc. etc.," Moynihan wrote. "The liberal Left will acknowledge the relevance of these facts only to the extent that they serve as an indictment of American society."

Moynihan's bitterness was unmistakable. So was his air of certitude. His principal grievance against Watts appeared to be that it had spoiled his policy initiative. He did not entertain the possibility that the policy itself might be mistimed or misconceived. And he said very little about Vietnam, the event that had done most to reorder LBJ's priorities.

Moynihan's analysis implied there could be no honest disagreement with him, or with the social science that informed his thinking. This in turn suggested that Great Society doctrine had attained the status of quasi-official scripture. And perhaps it had. In June 1967, Theodore H. White, the period's most admired political reporter, and its presidential laureate, composed (for *Life* magazine) an extended ode to the Johnson administration's brain trust in language so rapturous it reads today like satire. White extolled "the new priesthood, unique to this country and this time, of action-intellectuals"—social scientists "nominated by history to explain how communities shall master the changes provoked by the physical scientists and economists" and who patriotically "feel it is their duty to call down the heavy artillery on the targets they alone can see moving in the distance." Some were now grooved on a regular commutation track, from their ivied cells in the "Boston power-center of Harvard and M.I.T." to the Beltway, and back again. Meanwhile, money flowed from the government to the campuses. The new elite really seemed to be running things. The president himself was little more than "a transmission belt, packaging and processing scholars' ideas to be sold to Congress as program." The delighted front man for the managerial elite, Johnson had ordered a head count of all the credentialed scholars on his payroll. White faithfully reported the results: "five Rhodes scholars at top level, 77 intellectuals badged with a Phi Beta Kappa key (five in the Cabinet, one in the White House, one in the legislative branch, 13 ambassadors, 23 in sub-Cabinet positions, 29 appointed in independent or regulatory agencies, five as bureau chiefs), plus 33 major appointments fresh from professorships and 40 more with other specific scholarly background." Summoned to the epicenter of power, "the new priesthood" busily served its sacerdotal purpose, building heaven on earth, ministering to the whole range of human wants and psychological needs. The "action-intellectuals" gamboled "across disciplines—in economics and psychology, in health and psychiatry, in images and heritages, in arithmetic and beauty."

Like so much celebratory journalism, White's report was already out-of-date. The idyllic campuses were fast becoming battlegrounds, sites of sit-ins, teach-ins, antiwar protests. Students were in open revolt against administrators and faculties who colluded with the Pentagon on secret research projects. Others were organizing demands for new curriculums more responsive to the counterculture. In the summer of 1967, not quite four weeks after the third of White's articles appeared, with its assurances that the "action-intellectuals" were hard at work "redesigning our cities," one of the most afflicted, Newark, was spontaneously redesigned by rampaging rioters. The city would never recover. A week later Detroit went up in flames. The mobs were subdued only after LBJ sent in seventeen thousand law enforcement troops—including forty-seven hundred U.S. Army paratroopers. The casualties resembled the Vietnam statistics scrolled on the nightly news: 43 people killed, 467 injured; there were more than seven thousand arrests, and some two thousand buildings burned to the ground.

By this time the public's "conservative bias" had already asserted itself. In the congressional elections of 1966 Republicans won forty-seven seats in the House, a clear rebuke to the Great Society and "the new priesthood," who were also dragging the country deeper into Vietnam. This shift has recently been interpreted as the incipient stage of a new reactionary politics. In his essay "The Fall of Conservatism," published in *The New Yorker* in 2008, George Packer described the election through the eyes of the Republican presidential hopeful Richard Nixon, who as he stumped for GOP candidates was looking ahead to 1968 and "saw that he could propel himself back to power on the strength of a new feeling among Americans who, appalled by the chaos of the cities, the moral heedlessness of the young, and the insults to national pride in Vietnam, were ready to blame it all on the liberalism of President Lyndon B. Johnson." These angry whites included "the kind of men whom Nixon whipped into a frenzy one night in the fall of 1966" in a hotel in Columbia, South Carolina, in a room "full of sweat, cigar smoke, and rage." The evening's "rhetoric, which was about patriotism and law and order, 'burned the paint off the walls.' " The result? "In November the Republicans won a midterm landslide."

Actually, the big Republican winners in 1966 were not rednecks or rabble-rousers or archconservatives. They were centrists and progressives, the senators Charles Percy (Illinois), Howard Baker (Tennessee), Robert Griffin (Michigan), Mark Hatfield (Oregon), and Edward Brooke (Massachusetts), the first African American elected to the chamber since Reconstruction. In Maryland's election for governor, the segregationist Democrat George P. Mahoney ("Your Home Is Your Castle—Defend It") lost to the centrist Republican Spiro T. Agnew. Together the victors composed "a new generation of young, moderate Republicans," as *The New York Times* put it in an editorial.

Conservative alarms about the New Deal were beginning to sound like prophecies about Great Society hubris. In the 1950s, Buckley, Bozell, and, in his way, Joe McCarthy had accused the consensus ideal of being the opposite of what it claimed—not the meeting ground of convergent views but in fact its own closed system of belief, intolerant of dissent. Buckley had repeated the warning at the outset of the Kennedy years. "I am obliged to confess," he had written in 1960, "that I should sooner live in a society governed by the first two thousand names in the Boston telephone directory than in a society governed by the two thousand faculty members of Harvard University." Buckley went on:

> Not, heaven knows, because I hold lightly the brainpower or knowledge or generosity or even the affability of the Harvard faculty: but because I greatly fear intellectual arrogance, and that is a distinguishing characteristic of the university which refuses to accept any common premise. In the deliberations of two thousand citizens of Boston I think one would discern a respect for the laws of God and for the wisdom of our ancestors which does not characterize the thought of Harvard professors—who, to the extent that they believe in God at all, tend to believe He made some terrible mistakes which they would undertake to rectify; and, when they are paying homage to the wisdom of our ancestors, tend to do so with a kind of condescension toward those whose accomplishments we long since surpassed.

It wasn't just right-wingers who were saying this. The social critic Paul Goodman, whose book *Growing Up Absurd* was a favorite text of the New Left, suspected that Great Society gigantism concealed totalitarian designs. "We must note the change in slogans," he wrote in *The New York Review of Books* in October 1965, two months after Watts. " 'Fair Deal' and 'New Deal' used to refer to political economy and were a legitimate bid for votes; 'New Frontier' and 'Great Society' are more spiritual . . . The concept of a national mission . . . is not merely a fraud. It is an ideology." Goodman's critique of the establishment, particularly its reliance on a "large stable of mandarins to raise the tone, use correct scientific method, and invent rationalization," echoed James Burnham's claim that ideology itself was the political equivalent of " 'rationalization' in the sphere of individual psychology." And just as Burnham theorized that the managerial elite was covertly advancing Marxism, so Goodman warned that the new priesthood was betraying the legitimate goals of a responsible politics. "Instead of tackling the political puzzle of how to maintain democracy in a complex technology and among urban masses, it multiplies professional-client and patron-client relationships."

Burke, it was true, had said government was contrived to furnish "human wants"—that is, whatever people couldn't furnish for themselves. But this formulation had come in the early stages of the Industrial Revolution, before it was clear that a vibrant federally supported market could itself satisfy many of those wants. In times of emergency, like the Great Depression, the government had every reason to reassert its strength. But if government assumed such power in an age of abundance, as the 1960s decidedly were, it threatened to sap individual initiative and, even worse, create dependency in its "clients," who would expect an unceasing flow of gratification. But what happened when people's wants, as they multiplied, began to conflict?

It was possible to hear in this the echo not only of Burnham but also of Herbert Hoover, who had said the danger of "big government" inhered not in all the bad things it threatened to do *to* us but in the surplus of good things it promised to do *for* us. The argument could be traced back further still: to John Stuart Mill, who had warned (in his classic *On Liberty*) that "the absorption of all the principal ability of the country into the governing body is fatal, sooner or later, to the mental activity and progressiveness of the body itself," not least because it threatened to cancel the influence of autonomous critics and monitors, a vital presence "if we would not have our bureaucracy degenerate into a pedantocracy."

In 1972, David Halberstam would pin the phrase "the best and the brightest" on the Kennedy-Johnson brain trust, its Ivy-trained "organization men"—the efficiency experts and market researchers, the bold, outside-the-box "ideas men." The most driven planner in JFK's cabinet, his defense secretary, Robert McNamara, the number-crunching prodigy of the Ford Motor Company, rigorously applied systems analysis to Pentagon spending, and under LBJ conducted the Vietnam War as a kind of research-and-development project, complete with statistical models. The result: years of futile conflict and millions dead. "Pure logic," as George Santayana observed in *Scepticism and Animal Faith,* his critique of pragmatism, has "no necessary application to anything." Even what seems the most rigorous ratiocinative thought becomes a form of faith, for once "we assert that one thing is more probable than another . . . we profess to have some hold on the nature of things at large, a law seems to us to rule events."

In September 1967, Moynihan, who had left the government and was now director of the Joint Center for Urban Studies at MIT and Harvard, spoke at a two-day meeting in Washington of the Americans for Democratic Action (ADA) and startled his listeners with a mea culpa that made the front page of *The New York Times.* "Liberals must divest themselves of the notion that the nation, especially the cities of the nation, can be run from agencies in Washington," Moynihan said. These words shifted the familiar antigovernment attack to new ground—away from entrenched bureaucracies and toward the inventive new enclaves of policy innovation and "community action" programs. It was an early expression of what would come to be known as neoconservatism. Moynihan also ominously warned his liberal audience to "prepare for the onset of terrorism" in a society that seemed to be losing its moorings. Most important, liberals must rethink a central premise: Government programs might not work. Washington "is good at collecting revenues, and rather bad at disbursing services." The sums being squandered in Washington should go to state and local governments. What's more, liberals, instead of assigning blame to others for the current crisis in the cities, should acknowledge that "more than anyone else it is they who have been in office, in power at the time of, and in large measure presided over," the upsurge of urban rioting, which came "in the aftermath of one of the most extraordinary periods of liberal electoral victories that we have ever experienced." Liberals also must "see more clearly that their essential interest is in the stability of the social order, and that, given the present threats to that stability, it is necessary to seek out and make much more effective alliances with political conservatives who share that concern, and who recognize that unyielding rigidity is just as much a threat to the continuity of things as is an anarchic desire for change." The speech, titled "The Politics of Stability," was pure Edmund Burke—rather, Burke filtered through England's leading contemporary conservative thinker, Michael Oakeshott, whom Moynihan had been reading.

"Anything we conservatives can do to help, just holler," William Buckley wrote in his syndicated column. He offered his own gloss on Moynihan: "So serious is the crisis that liberals have to decide whether, as the New Left believes, liberalism is about to go up in smoke, ushering in a new ideology, or whether liberalism can tuck away its superstitions and get down to the nitty-gritty of achieving stability and progress."

Buckley betrayed no delight in liberalism's "crisis." Why should he since the nation itself was in jeopardy? He had been giving serious thought to Whittaker Chambers's admonitions on the necessity of pragmatic maneuver: "how much to give in order not to give up the basic principles." Buckley himself had been maneuvering energetically. He was intent now on guiding the Right closer to the center. In 1965, he programmatically assailed the John Birch Society, first denouncing Welch's "drivel" in his column and then, with Burnham, editing a special issue of *National Review* condemning not just Welch but the entire organization, over the protests of other staff. Buckley received a shower of hate mail from angry subscribers. But he was on firm ground, having obtained support in advance from leading political figures, including Goldwater, Reagan, and Senator John Tower, who read Buckley's columns into the *Congressional Record* and made a statement defending them on the Senate floor.

At the same time, Buckley had been schooling himself in practical politics. In 1965 he had run for mayor of New York City on the ticket of the upstart Conservative Party, challenging the presumptive favorite, John Lindsay, a congressman from Manhattan's Silk Stocking District who had secured both the Republican and Liberal party endorsements. Lindsay, though anathema to the Right, was being discussed as presidential material, a paladin of progressive Republicanism. He envisioned a municipal Great Society. During the campaign he had recruited bank analysts to study the city's economy, management consultants to parse city hall operations, professors of medievalism to contrive designs for beautifying the waterfront and public spaces. Theodore White, in his *Life* series, tallied up the Lindsay eggheads. "No fewer than 17 college deans, professors and lecturers to his staff. 'If you got together all the books they'd written,' says an old city hall hand, 'they'd fill every shelf in this room.' "

Buckley, meanwhile, avid to establish that conservative ideas could be applied to the "crisis in the cities"—began seriously examining urban issues, from crime to pollution to declining property values. He wrote all his own speeches and all his position papers—at night and on weekends, in between editing *National Review,* producing three syndicated columns a week, honoring his lecture commitments, with a week off to compete in a sailing race to Halifax. Eventually, he had covered, sometimes imaginatively, every major issue, from water (he proposed a free-market solution) to business taxes (he recommended a European-style "value added tax"), unions (end the closed shop), and transit and traffic (install bicycle lanes). At one point, he sent a letter to Walt Disney suggesting he erect a "Disneyland East" on the site of the World's Fair when it ceased operations in October.

But it was Buckley's tough stances on crime and welfare that attracted voters. Though he failed to capture any single district, he finished second in parts of Queens and did especially well among Irish and German Catholics who had once been reliable

Democrats. "There is no real precedent in American politics for the kind of wrecking operation that Buckley is conducting," Walter Lippmann wrote in his column. Soon "Goldwaterism" would be replaced by a new expression, "Buckleyism." When a *Times* editorial accused him of stoking racial antagonisms, Buckley pointed out that he had not said "a single thing about the Negro problem in Harlem that hasn't been said by others whom you have not, so far as I am aware, done one of your hippopotamus-walks over. Mr. Daniel Moynihan, for instance, whose credentials are by your standards in very good order."

Buckley's campaign, though initially treated as a lark—not least by himself—had actually built a sturdy bridge from Goldwater's rather crude movement-driven campaign in 1964 to the more sophisticated candidacy of Ronald Reagan, the landslide victor in the California governor's race in 1966. Reagan's political history capsuled the movement's progress. In the early 1960s, he had shared platforms with the segregationists Ross Barnett and Orval Faubus and stumped for his "warm personal friend" John Rousselot, a Southern California congressman who was the pride of the John Birch Society. In 1964, when Nelson Rockefeller had hired the California GOP consultants Stu Spencer and Bill Roberts to manage his campaign in the California primary, they ranked Reagan twenty-second on a list of Goldwater's "fringe backers," with the notation: "Another Liberty Amendment stalwart." After Goldwater's loss, Reagan decried the moderate GOP "traitors" who "are pledged to the same Socialist goals of our opposition." But by 1966 he had already moved beyond Goldwaterism. Although Reagan is ritually invoked today as the enemy of big government, voters in 1966 were attracted by his promise to strengthen the government in the Moynihan sense—as the institutional guarantor of "stability" against student demonstrators and urban rioters.

The import of Reagan's victory was captured by Richard Goodwin, another fugitive from the Great Society—in fact Moynihan's collaborator on Johnson's Howard University speech, though he had since broken with LBJ over Vietnam and moved to the left.

In "The Shape of American Politics," published in *Commentary* in June 1967, Goodwin described the 1966 election as a referendum on the federal Leviathan. The vote "dramatized yet another important responsibility now assigned to government: keeper of the status quo. It is expected to be the protector of all those who are both delighted and unsure about their new affluence—the suburban houses, new cars, and television sets. They command the government to restrain any social turbulence which seems to threaten their personal position." Amid the upheavals of the 1960s, citizens wanted government—specifically the federal government—to exert the authority Burke and Disraeli had claimed for it. This, Goodwin wrote, was the essence of "Reaganism."

Like Moynihan, Goodwin was a transitional figure. He combined the anti-authoritarian sentiments of the New Left—and its ideal of politics as the vehicle of a universalizing personal "authenticity"—with the conservative belief in self-sovereignty. He lamented "the most troubling political fact of our age: that the growth in central power has been accompanied by a swift and continual diminution in the significance of the individual citizen, transforming him from a wielder into an object of authority," and a dependent one, too. "The federal government spends one-seventh of our national wealth and creates more of it. Between 1950 and 1960, nine out of ten new jobs were created by the public and the private not-for-profit sectors, and only one out of ten by private enterprise." All this placed too heavy a burden on Washington: "It is the government, not private business, that is held responsible for the conditions of the economy: credited with prosperity; blamed for recession and inflation; expected simultaneously to make the country prosper, end unemployment, and keep prices down . . . it is also expected to ensure justice." But the system wasn't built to do all that. The answer lay in decentralization. Goodwin found a shred of hope in one place: Buckley's mayoral campaign. Instead of appealing to the federal government, Buckley "argued for city action against problems ranging from air pollution to the scarcity of bicycle paths . . . he opposed federal intervention because it was 'none of their business,' making his objections to government action more geographical than ideological."

By virtue of his celebrity—the mayoral campaign and *Firing Line,* the television debate show it spawned—Buckley had become America's most famous conservative and, now, a Burkean one. In the disorderly 1960s it made no sense for conservatives to attack "statism" when it was institutions of the State that formed the bedrock of civil society. In 1967, when Reagan, soon after his election, was being accused of having sold out his antigovernment principles—not least because he had submitted the highest budget in state history—Buckley wondered what exactly critics expected Reagan to do, "padlock the state treasury and give speeches on the Liberty amendment?"

Buckley also became an unexpected defender of LBJ. Buckley adamantly opposed the Great Society. Its "pretensions," he would later write, "like the ideals of the Allies in World War I, 'grew grander with every restatement of them.' Johnson was going to do something about the quality of our lives!" But Buckley was ardently pro–Vietnam War and appalled when protesters taunted Johnson with cries that he was a murderous war criminal. "We are being invited to despise not merely Johnson's policies, not merely Johnson's style, but Johnson's person," Buckley wrote in April 1968. "And to feel proud of ourselves for doing so. In the name of humanity, you understand." Buckley was indignant when "the Kids" harried their liberal professors and heckled Buckley himself when he gave visiting lectures. When Democrats rallied behind the "Dump Johnson" movement, Buckley objected that it was politics by coup and a threat to orderly democratic procedures, even though the GOP benefited from the infighting.

In April 1968, a strong challenge by Eugene McCarthy in the New Hampshire primary prompted Johnson to abandon a reelection campaign. Some on the right rejoiced. But not Buckley. "This is an important datum," he wrote in his column shortly after Johnson's announcement.

Some will hail it as evidence that The People are in better command of their own affairs. Others, conservatives for the most part, will wonder whether it is all a cause for rejoicing. The conservative fears plebiscitary government, for the very reasons given by [Edmund] Burke and [John] Adams. Instant guidance by the people of the government means instability, and instability is subversive of freedom. If Lyndon Johnson has to step down because 45 percent of the Democrats in New Hampshire, half of them unable to reply accurately to the question whether Senator McCarthy was for or against the Vietnam War, voted for McCarthy, and because thousands of college students moo over Bobby Kennedy . . . there is something somehow unsettling about it all.

Nineteen sixty-eight was a cataclysmic year, marked by two political assassinations and a series of riots. Moynihan's prediction of "terrorism" seemed plausible. Buckley, deploying Burkean terms, affirmed the need to maintain social order, even if it meant preserving the welfare state. Weeks before the two national conventions were held (each eclipsed by a riot), Buckley wrote a column based on a remark Gerry Bush, a young operative in Hubert Humphrey's campaign, had made to a British journalist. "We can win the election in November," he had said, "but then can we govern the country?" Buckley interviewed Bush and reported that Bush's "stated worries were by no means confined to the difficulties that a Humphrey administration would have in governing the country. He meant that the serious question has arisen: Can *anyone* govern the country?" The trouble was coming from the Left. "If Hubert Humphrey is elected President, the followers of Richard Nixon and Ronald Reagan are not going to start burning down their Union League clubs or their Masonic lodges," Buckley wrote. "But some of the followers of Eugene McCarthy are, as some of them have put it, disposed to burn, baby, burn. Does this mean that the unruly left has maneuvered into a position whence blackmail is effectively exerted? Vote our man—or else we shall disrupt the republic?"

The beneficiary of all this discord was the Republican candidate, Richard Nixon, who organized a ruthlessly efficient campaign. Today we remember Nixon's harshly polarizing tactics—the Faustian bargain of his "southern strategy," including his courtship of Strom Thurmond and other Old South segregationists, which played on white resistance to civil rights legislation; the coded appeals to "law and order" aimed at restive urban ethnics. But Nixon the candidate was careful to calm, not stoke, national anxieties. He ran on his generalized affinity with Middle America, "the silent majority," and diligently adhered to the thin script of " 'play-it-safe' campaigning," in the opinion of Samuel Lubell, skirting all divisive policy debates. "He minimized the risk of saying anything which might offend anybody," Arthur Schlesinger Jr. wrote in *The New York Times Magazine.* The approach might be unsatisfying, but the moment called for it, as Nixon well knew. A maestro of the political arts, he exhibited a conspicuous talent for maneuver, apparent from the outset of his career. It made him one of the most accomplished vote-getters in history, a phenomenon who appeared on his first national ticket, as Eisenhower's running mate, at age thirty-nine. Even as vice president, sealed inside another man's administration, Nixon was "breathtakingly adaptable," Richard Rovere observed in 1955, his views "indeterminate and perhaps nonexistent."

Struggling to unlock the mystery of Nixon's appeal, Rovere located it in his persona, so routinely despised today. "The admirers admire Richard Nixon himself," Rovere concluded. "As a person and as a personality, he embodies much that is held to be precious by a large and growing number of Americans—especially in that segment of the middle class to which he belongs and which is recognized by the Republican party as its best source of cadres at the present . . . His general appearance, his dress, his whole style of living and being, commend him to the multitudes."

All this enabled Nixon, even as he deployed the strategy of "positive polarization," to soothe the raging passions of 1968—to restore the nation to a happier vision, or memory, of itself. Yet Nixon's victory was among the least decisive in modern history. He won only 43 percent of the popular vote, the smallest plurality of any elected president since Woodrow Wilson in 1912. And Nixon was the first president since Zachary Taylor in 1849 to take office with both houses of Congress controlled by the opposition party.

And what of the 57 percent who had not voted for Nixon—in particular the 13.5 percent, or nearly ten million voters, who had chosen the third-party spoiler George Wallace? Had they, too, voted for "stability"? Richard Goodwin, writing in *The New Yorker* in January 1969, as Nixon prepared to take office, suspected not. Both the Left and the Right were more estranged than ever from "the 'power structure,' " and Middle Americans, as they were coming to be called, were, too. The "urban white" voter, for one, had become alienated, his discontent "fed both by envy of the more prosperous and by anger at the blacks—not just because he fears the blacks but also because their problems, and not his, seem to be the focus of national concern." The Democratic sun had imploded. But had the Republican moon really become a sun?

Sifting through the election results in *Nixon Agonistes*, Garry Wills wrote liberalism's epitaph in the vocabulary he had honed in a decade of writing for *National Review*, now the lingua franca of mainstream political discourse: "The liberal Eastern Establishment found it was not needed on election day—which made its leaders take a second look at the Forgotten American, at an angry baffled middle class that, paying the bill for progress, found its values mocked by spokesmen for that progress. These voters felt cheated, disregarded, robbed of respect; and unless their support could be reenlisted, the Establishment's brand of liberalism would perish as a political force."

What had been lost in the 1960s was belief in authority itself, in its capacity to maintain social order. Conservatives now promised to do that. But what order did they intend to uphold? "Although established liberalism certainly has deep ideological responsibility for nihilist radicalism," the columnist Frank S. Meyer wrote in *National Review* in 1970, "it has also been the governing form of the social order in this country for the past forty years." The Right had become the guardian of all it had once pledged to undo.

4

THE NEW CLASS AND
OLD ENMITIES

The repudiation of the Great Society combined with the Right's new sophistication seemed to promise a new period in U.S. politics, one in which conservatives, fortified by Burkean principles, might emerge as the most articulate voices of "civil society," separating out the strands of true reform, which drew on inherited values, from "liberal-left" attempts to make those values extinct.

In any event, after a thirty-six-year cycle of eclipse, conservatives would now be responsible for administering the government and held accountable for the results. Denouncing the excesses of big government was easy as long as the denouncers exercised no power. But now the Republicans were expected to attend to the conflicting array of "human wants," either by re-configuring the calculus of "patron-client" relationships or by finding a workable substitute for them. This could not be done through the "abstract rule" of ideology, in Burke's phrase. Conservatives, and the Nixon administration in particular, must adjust to changing "times and circumstances" and also "admit of infinite modifications" in their thinking. And the place to begin was with the sputtering engine of the market, more entangled than ever with the operations of government.

Nixon initially seemed eager to reformulate, and even reform, the relationship between the two. This may seem surprising, since Nixon today permanently inhabits the netherworld of our political history, summoned only for punishment—by the Left for his bitter declaration of war on "the liberal media" and for his secret bombing of Cambodia; by the Right for his Machiavellian courtship of Communist China and for Soviet détente and his determined enlargement of the federal government; and by everyone, more or less, for Watergate and its unparalleled misprisions.

Yet Nixon's gifts were prodigious. No modern president surpassed him in sheer ability—intellectual or political. As he assumed his presidential duties in 1969, his lack of a mandate seemed a potential advantage. Having promised so little, he was committed to even less. His objective was to duplicate Roosevelt's feat of building a durable new majority—and he would eventually achieve one that far outlasted the "permanent" majority Karl Rove foretold in 2004.

But if Nixon was little touched by ideology, he did have an idea. He told journalists he had been reading Richard Goodwin and Daniel Patrick Moynihan, and was much impressed by their prescriptions for "decentralization"—possible blueprints for a "new federalism" that would restore governing power to the states and localities. In fact, Nixon had been courting Moynihan since the ADA speech in 1967 and lured him with the job of "counselor to the president on urban affairs," an ad hoc cabinet-level position. Moynihan's liberal admirers, at least the few who remained, were dismayed. But Moynihan and Nixon fascinated each other. "Daniel Patrick Moynihan bloomed in 1969's spring, with his Disraeli books [including Robert Blake's recent biography] and shibboleth-shattering ideas," William Safire writes in his memoir, *Before the Fall.* "Nixon was in love . . . Moynihan was in [the Oval Office] for long hours, taking Nixon to the mountaintop of social psychology and showing him vistas of Rooseveltian glories."

Despite his reputation for being a hard-liner, Safire adds, Nixon was "a progressive politician, willing and even eager to surprise with liberal ideas, [and he was] delighted with the comparison" to Disraeli, a conservative who had governed innovatively, outflanking liberals. It was the politics of maneuver, but anchored in moral realism. "The people have their passions," Disraeli said in 1834 at the outset of his public career, "and it is even the duty of public men occasionally to adopt sentiments with which they do not sympathize, because the people must have leaders."

Passions were boiling in 1969—conflicting passions, boiling at different temperatures. Which, or whose, should Nixon attend to? The election offered few clues. To build a majority, Nixon would have to lure Wallace voters back to the center or persuade them he was on their side. Kevin Phillips, a twenty-nine-year-old lawyer who had expertly analyzed the ethnic vote for the Nixon campaign, believed it was already happening. In his book *The Emerging Republican Majority,* he outlined—with maps, charts, and graphs—a massive realignment reflecting "a populist revolt of the American masses who have been elevated by prosperity to middle-class status and conservatism. *Their* revolt is against the caste, policies and taxation of the mandarins of the Establishment liberalism." The 1968 election was merely the prelude to 1972, when Wallace voters became Republicans, creating the foundation of a "new populist coalition." Democratic liberalism would recover, but as a moon to the Republican sun, "injecting a needed leavening of humanism into the middle-class *realpolitik* of the new Republican coalition," Phillips predicted.

Nixon's very drabness had the virtue of draining anger from politics and drawing diverse constituents to the common ground of a new consensus that might yield a "combination of the reforming spirit with the conservative ideal," in the words of Irving Kristol, co-editor of *The Public Interest*, the quarterly that had established itself as the new beachhead of a post–Great Society politics. The prospect for conjoining reform and conservatism was the subject of "Capitalism Today," a special issue of *The Public Interest* published in 1970.

In an ambitious essay, "The Cultural Contradictions of Capitalism," Kristol's co-editor Daniel Bell described the rise of the "adversary culture"—a phrase he borrowed from Lionel Trilling—with its postmodernist sensibility, its distrust of authority and the "bourgeois world-view," and the parallel rise of countercultural excess, and concluded that both derived from the irresistible push of market capitalism. "New buying habits in a high consumption economy" in the postindustrial age had caused the "erosion of the Protestant Ethic and the Puritan Temper," and with it had "undercut the beliefs and legitimations that sanctioned work and reward in American society."

In other words, the market had created a generation of consumers of the Rolling Stones and *I Am Curious (Yellow)*, and had mass-produced the automobiles in which teenagers discovered sex to soundtracks that poured forth from radios. All this suggested that the authors of social disruption weren't Harvard mandarins or salaried managers in the State Department and the Department of Health, Education, and Welfare. They were nestled instead in corporate America, in the honeycombed cells of what John Kenneth Galbraith called "the technostructure" of "the new industrial state."

How could it be otherwise in a society that hymned the purifying virtues of the profit motive? The Great Society might be guilty of trying to satisfy too many "wants," but it was the free market that had planted those wants in the first place, nourishing fresh appetites and an insatiable "desire for the new." There was nothing intrinsically wrong with this. The trouble was that America's business elite had "abdicated" its obligation to reconcile modernizing impulses with traditional values and so was complicit in fostering a contemporary counterculture in which "antinomianism and anti-institutionalism rule."

How, then, to restore national belief in civil society and its high values? In an essay offering "reflections on capitalism and 'the free society,'" Kristol tried to parse the most saliently estranged segment of the population, the young, who abhorred American displays of power yet forgave the authoritarian excesses of Castro's Cuba. It was easy to label them ignorant or anti-American. But this didn't address the important question: *Why* did the young feel alienated from their country and its traditions? Kristol, like Bell, pointed to "the dynamics of capitalism itself," which had created "the inner spiritual chaos of the times" and so made "nihilism an easy temptation." The evi-

dence could be found in "extreme libertarian" economists like
F. A. Hayek and Milton Friedman, latter-day utilitarians. When
Friedman maintained that the ideal citizen in a free society "rec-
ognizes no national purpose except as it is the consensus of the
purposes for which the citizenry severally strive," he meant not
consensus "but rather the mere aggregation of selfish aims."

Kristol found more useful guidance in two humanist intellectuals of the industrial era, Matthew Arnold and Herbert
Croly, each "a liberal reformer with essentially conservative
goals." In his essay "Democracy," Arnold, a contemporary of
Disraeli, had argued that the national government, though it
could do little for the "highest and richest class of its people, can
really do much, by institution and regulation, to better [the con-
dition] of the middle and lower classes. The State can bestow
certain broad collective benefits, which are indeed not much if
compared with the advantages already possessed by individual
grandeur, but which are rich and valuable if compared with the
make-shifts of mediocrity and poverty." Croly, in his book *The
Promise of American Life,* had exposed the emptiness of free-
market liturgy and its corollary belief that moral and social benefits could be achieved "merely by liberating the enlightened
self-enterprise of the American people."

What America needed, Kristol proposed, was a renewed "national purpose" that could overcome "the ideological barren-
ness of the liberal and conservative creeds." Later in the decade,
Kristol expanded this argument, urging Republicans to give
"comprehensive thought to the question of what a *conservative
welfare state* would look like" since, to be realistic, "the idea of a
welfare state is in itself perfectly consistent with a conservative
political philosophy . . . In our urbanized, industrialized, highly

mobile society, people need governmental action of some kind if they are to cope with many of their problems: old age, illness, unemployment, etc. They need such assistance; they demand it; they will get it."

It was exactly the case Whittaker Chambers had made to Buckley twenty years before, only Chambers had concluded that the welfare state as it then existed already served conservative ends. It fostered the politics of stability by narrowing the gaps between "the islands of relative plenty" and "the continents of proliferating poverty."

Many have pointed out that Nixon consistently departed from movement antigovernment doctrine. He created the Environmental Protection Agency, instated affirmative-action hiring programs, and openly endorsed Keynesian stimulus. But his first and boldest initiative came on the issue of poverty, with encouragement from Moynihan. It took the pair only six months to contrive a program that updated the Disraelian ideal of a blended radicalism and conservatism even as it revived Moynihan's thwarted family policy. Called the Family Assistance Plan, it proposed a national "minimum floor" income, which meant direct cash transfers to the 8.5 million people on welfare rolls. The handouts would be made by the individual states, but the federal government would supply the money and also coordinate disbursements.

More radically still, the Family Assistance Plan also included payments to the working poor—in violation of the sacred principle that subsidies for the employed would lull them into quitting their jobs. But Moynihan was looking elsewhere, at the tangle of pathology, the cycle of disintegrating families. Many states refused payments to households where an adult male was living. As a result, women chose to live singly rather than give up their welfare payments, and families were sundered. A cash supplement to workingmen would make them genuine bread-winners. The proposal also included mandatory job training, and day-care centers for working mothers.

To movement conservatives all this looked opportunistic or worse. Nixon had quelled their doubts in large part because he had stumped diligently in 1964 for Goldwater, the sworn enemy of the welfare state, and he had won the nomination in 1968 only after courting the Right. Now he was veering traitorously left. But Disraeli had an answer for that, too: the statesman, he had said, is "essentially a practical character; . . . the conduct and the opinions of public men at different periods of their ca-reer must not be too curiously contrasted in a free and aspiring country."

The grand experiment languished and then died. Like LBJ before him, Nixon became preoccupied with Vietnam, the dom-inant issue of his presidency. It was the liberals' war—the climax of their policy of Communist containment. But it had gone badly. How to end it without ceding ground in the Cold War struggle? Nixon's solution was brilliant twinned gambles—Soviet détente, which removed the necessity for a proxy super-power chess match, and his overtures to China, which lowered tensions in Southeast Asia and made possible the removal of American commitments there. It was global strategy on a scale unmatched by any president since.

And it worked. "By 1972 the original 1969 print-out tables of withdrawal that [Melvin] Laird still flourished in the office of the Secretary of Defense were dirty, dog-eared and tattered, but the targets had been met," Theodore White noted in *The Making of the President, 1972.* "From 549,500 to 524,500 to 484,000 to 434,000 to 284,000 to 184,000, the number of troops had fallen to 139,000 as election year opened. In 1968 and early 1969 it was not uncommon for 300 Americans to be killed in a week; by midsummer of 1972 the average had fallen to 3 or 4. Out There, Nixon had promised to get the boys home." The reward came in the next election. He assimilated the Wallace vote, as Kevin Phillips had predicted, and achieved one of the greatest landslides in history.

But then, five years to the day after his speech introducing the Family Assistance Plan, Nixon resigned amid the ruinous crimes of Watergate. The exemplar of the politics of stability had become its principal subverter. In Nixon revanchist impulses collided with realistic ones—and overwhelmed them. Even as he destroyed his own presidency, he released the furies of movement politics most conspicuously with us today.

Watergate, once uncovered and prosecuted, gave conservatives the ideal occasion to reassert their role as guardians of social order. It should have been easy to do. Movement ideologues had never trusted Nixon, in fact viewed him as an impostor, a secret liberal. Nixon's "betrayal of the conservatives," in the formulation of William Rusher, was a pet theme of the Right.

But just as liberals suspicious of Bill Clinton would rally behind him during his impeachment, so Nixon's Republican critics became his defenders during Watergate. The true culprit, they decided, wasn't Nixon. It was the dark liberal forces arrayed against him. A "long term change in the equation of political power," Jeffrey Hart theorized in *National Review,* had placed the president at the mercy of "the federal bureaucracy," which, "though nominally part of the 'executive branch,' actually operates with considerable autonomy."

For decades it was conservatives who had cautioned against the destabilizing dangers of overreaching "Caesarist" presidents. In his book *Congress and the American Tradition*, Burnham, revising his theory on elites, now depicted them as the agents not of their own class interests but of "executive supremacy," which reversed the intentions of the founders and their ideal of "localization," with its emphasis on the negotiation of differences within the House of Representatives, each member accountable to his sovereign constituents and chosen by them directly.

Burnham's book was published in 1959, when the Caesar was Eisenhower, who was in fact ill disposed to despotism and had tried to remove the mystique of the "indispensable man" from the presidency by routinizing executive authority through a system of hierarchy and established channels on the military model, with orders passed up and down the chain of command and clear lines of responsibility. It was Democratic presidents from Roosevelt on who had declared war on the "permanent government."

Burnham, true to his doctrine, was appalled by Watergate, especially after Nixon invoked executive privilege to evade congressional inquiry into "the shoddy little trail of this pipsqueak Watergate business," with "all the secrets, the hundred-dollar bills, . . . the spreading political paranoia that finds 'enemies' in every nook and cranny." Burnham also drafted the statement delivered by Senator James Buckley, William's brother, calling for Nixon to resign. George Will, *National Review* alumnus, was blunter still. "The Nixon White House ran amok as no other has done," he wrote in his syndicated column, "and its abuses were uniquely lurid and sinister."

But these were minority voices on the right. Others identified a second culprit, the "liberal-left bias of the major media," in Jeffrey Hart's phrase. There was some justice to this argument. Watergate had been the excrescence of Vietnam, particularly of the release of the Pentagon Papers, which to the Right seemed vengeance against Nixon's management of the war. Even as he brought the troops home, and even as the public supported his policies, he remained under constant attack, on editorial pages and in the nightly news. "The establishment has a guilt complex," Nixon told Edward Heath, the British prime minister. "They can't stand that I, their political opponent, am rectifying their mistakes." He retaliated by loosing his vice president, Spiro Agnew, on the press, a declaration of war that later delivered us Rush Limbaugh and Fox News, with its sardonic parody ("fair and balanced") of a "mainstream" media it assumes to be rife with contempt.

Through it all Watergate remained central to the emerging doctrine of both the Right and the Left and shaped their views of presidential power. For conservatives, the lesson was political. Nixon, a popular president who had been successfully managing a war begun by Democrats but now disowned by them, was ripe for punishment by the "elites" at *The Washington Post* and by congressional Democrats, and the "third-rate burglary" provided a convenient pretext. Liberals interpreted the event legally. Nixon, the most egregious of the imperial presidents, had criminally violated his oath of office and jeopardized the Constitution. The truth, perhaps, was an amalgam of the two. Watergate began with Nixon's authentic crimes, but its aftermath unfolded in an incontrovertibly political context. The Yale Law School professor Alexander Bickel, in an influential analysis published in *Commentary* in 1974, acknowledged that conservatives fairly objected that the case had resulted in "accountability by crisis, accountability by trauma, accountability tending to shade into retribution." But conservatives, he added, should also be alarmed at what the event signaled more broadly: "Watergate is evidence of a weakened capacity of our legal order to serve as a self-executing safeguard against this sort of abuse of power." Once again "ideological imperatives and personal loyalty prevailed over the norms and commands of the legal order." It had happened in the 1950s, when white southerners resisted the Supreme Court's rulings on desegregation, and again in the late 1960s, when "the radical Left" had disrupted courtroom proceedings. Now the abuses were centered in the White House.

And yet Watergate secured the ascendancy of movement revanchism. In the twenty-year period from 1968 to 1988, the Republicans captured four of the five presidential elections. The single defeat, in 1976, was remarkably narrow, given the circumstances: an unelected incumbent, Gerald Ford, who barely survived a challenge in the primaries—by Reagan, the Right's new tribune—lost by only two percentage points to a conservative southern Democrat and self-proclaimed outsider as much at odds with the Beltway elite as any movement Republican of the time.

The argument that political power emanated from an alliance of liberal government bureaucrats and a sympathetic press became a favorite theme in the movement's next phase, elaborated in neo-populist books like Phillips's *Mediacracy,* Patrick J. Buchanan's *Conservative Votes, Liberal Victories,* and Rusher's *The Making of the New Majority Party.* Assessing the burgeoning literature of "New Right" ideology, Jeane Kirkpatrick detected a unifying set of beliefs she found delusional:

> Among these are the idea that there exists in the electorate a hidden conservative majority; that the social division with the greatest potential political significance is not that between "haves" and "have-nots" but between the liberal elite and everybody else; that a realignment of the parties into two ideologically homogeneous groups is both desirable and likely; that the Republican party may not prove an effective institutional channel for the expression of truly conservative politics and should perhaps be abandoned; and that the principal obstacles to the conservative cause are the nation's media monopolies.

It was back to intra-party warfare, the most intense since the Goldwater crusade of 1964. Buchanan and Rusher, in particular, "were offended by the continuing presence in the Republican party of a liberal minority which, ideologically speaking, belonged on the other side," Kirkpatrick noted. So preoccupied with doctrinal purity, New Right analysts missed the real meaning of the country's rightward drift, which had almost nothing to do with movement ideology. It was true that "a large majority of American adults are conservative," Kirkpatrick acknowledged, but in the classical, not movement, sense, since "they are attached to the existing society and will support it against challenges to its legitimacy."

The classical conservative moment was dissipating, and not only among New Right populists. In 1975, the same year the manifestos by Phillip, Buchanan, and Rusher all were published, Irving Kristol, the onetime elegist of the nonideological "reforming spirit," joined forces with the New Right in an essay identifying a "new class" of liberal enemies. Its members were "not much interested in money but are keenly interested in power," Kristol wrote. "Power for what? Well, the power to shape our civilization—a power, which, in a capitalist system, is supposed to reside in the free market. The 'new class' wants to see much of this power redistributed to government, where they will then have a major say in how it is exercised." And who, exactly, populated this new class? "Scientists, teachers and educational administrators, journalists and others in the communication industries, psychologists, social workers, those lawyers and doctors who make their careers in the expanding public sector, city planners, the staffs of the larger foundations, the upper levels of the government bureaucracy."

This formulation mirrored the "antinomianism and anti-institutionalism" Daniel Bell had attributed to the countercultural Left. It demonized government and society alike. The Right, it appeared, was nursing its own version of anti-Americanism, and this change eventually opened a chasm between Kristol and Bell. As Garry Wills, who broke with the movement in the 1970s but continued to call himself a conservative, observed in his memoir *Confessions of a Conservative* (1979): "The right wing in America is stuck with the paradox of holding a philosophy of 'conserving' an actual order it does not want to conserve."

The attack on the "new class," rooted in cultural hostility, dominated movement conservatism for the next thirty years, a period in which consensus all but disappeared from American politics. Kristol, once so critical of libertarian economics, with its ethos of greed, became an apostle of supply-side economics—lightening the tax burden on the rich in the faith, or hope, that the poor would be taken care of, the same argument Wall Street plutocrats had made in 1930.

The tribune of this new polarity was Ronald Reagan, whose denunciations of "big government" and the underclass it coddled—through "entitlements" and "giveaways"—were softened by his soothing assurances to those "delighted and unsure about their new affluence," as Richard Goodwin put it in 1967, no less dependent than the poor and unwilling to give up budget-draining "insurance" policies like Social Security and Medicare. In *Dead Right,* his withering deconstruction of the Reagan years, David Frum notes that "not one major spending program was abolished during the Reagan presidency. Only one spending program of any size was done away with, and even that—the worthless Comprehensive Employment and Training Act—was instantly replaced by another program, the Jobs Partnership Training Act, meant to achieve almost exactly the same end."

As Reagan's first term approached its end, it "has achieved as yet hardly anything in bringing the most rapidly growing domestic programs under control," Nathan Glazer concluded in *The Public Interest,* after examining the available budget data. The boom had been lowered in only one place. "The advocates of the poor play no role in this administration," Glazer found. "From this fact one can conclude that a certain blindness to their problems at best, and a positive malice at worst, animates the administration's policies." Reagan extended Nixon's "middle American" consensus but with no compensating acknowledgment of the Beaconsfield position.

Even Reagan's admirer George Will questioned the emerging romance with market capitalism that came to dominate the 1980s. "Conservatives rightly defend the market as a marvelous mechanism for allocating resources," Will wrote in *Statecraft as Soulcraft,* his Burkean defense of government, published in 1983. "But when conservatives begin regarding the market less as an expedient than as an ultimate value, or the ultimate arbiter of all values, their conservatism degenerates into the least conservative political impulse, which is populism. After all, the market is the judgment of 'the people' at any moment." But government, "unlike an economic market, has responsibilities," Will pointed out, and these included providing for the poor through "policies that express the community's acceptance of an ethic of common provision."

With Reagan, conservatism's argument with itself was presumed to have ended since his coalition drew on every faction of the ideological Right, including its new base of evangelicals. To this day movement conservatives continue the search for the new Reagan who will unite the movement's disparate components and heal its spiritual wounds. This was almost painfully apparent during the 2008 campaign. The pattern was established in the first Republican debate, held in the hangar of the Reagan Presidential Library, the ten candidates, gesticulating figurines, lined up beneath the gleaming immensity of Air Force One.

Reagan does indeed cast a large shadow. It was under him that movement doctrine achieved at last the status of conventional wisdom. By 1982, even Theodore White, the onetime rhapsodist of the action-intellectuals, was caricaturing federal agencies as "collectives of time servers . . . true bureaucrats" bent on "establishing behavioral patterns in a nation that previously had thought behavior best left to local community judgment."

The surprise was Reagan himself. He proved less an ideologue than his champions, often to their dismay. The distorting glow of nostalgia has made it all but impossible to find today a hard-core early Reaganite who admits having been disappointed by the affable mien Reagan later adopted, or by the many compromises he made as president: the massive deficits, the programs he promised to slash but never did, the crimes of Iran-contra, the friendly tête-à-têtes with Mikhail Gorbachev. But Reagan's signal accomplishment, his careful management of the Cold War's denouement, followed the example of strong rhetoric matched with flexible compromise set by Truman, Eisenhower, and Kennedy. At the time, however, movement intellectuals were incensed. Charles Krauthammer ridiculed Reagan's expedient pursuit of a profit-driven "what's good for General Motors" approach, which included removing sanctions Jimmy Carter had placed on the Soviet Union after it invaded Afghanistan. Norman Podhoretz voiced the displeasure of neoconservatives who "were cheering for Ronald Reagan" in 1980 but were "sinking into a state of near political despair" two years later.

This criticism echoed the one made three decades before when a staunch anti-Communist, James Burnham, deplored "the suicidal mania" of American businessmen eager to "trade with the enemy." But if the conflict between the two superpowers was also the struggle between two competing systems, why not conduct the war in "the marketplace," where America held the advantage? And if the tactical arsenal included psycho-logical warfare aimed at capturing "the hearts and minds" of other, watching nations, why not invite those nations to observe America's generosity and economic strength? This was the approach Eisenhower favored, hampered though he was by roll-back enthusiasts thirsting to foment civil war in China or to "liberate" the Soviet Union's satellite nations. Yet it was negotiation and compromise that finally ended the Cold War. Reagan understood this better than his disappointed critics.

In fact, it was disappointment with Reagan and anger at the presumed betrayals of his successor, George H. W. Bush—chosen by Reagan himself—that fed the bitterness of the 1990s, when conservatism entered its most decadent phase. The movement's new Danton, Newt Gingrich, who became Speaker of the House in 1995, proposed "reforms"—term limits for representatives, the purging of moderates from committee chairmanships—that would have mystified a conservative like Willmoore Kendall, who had contended that Congress's strength derived in large part from its institutional traditions. Meanwhile, Gingrich, and the House's Robespierre, Tom DeLay, tried to delegitimize a popular president, Bill Clinton, and assembled a shadow government of lobbyists who gained increasing influence over the legislative business of Congress.

During the Clinton years, right-wing intellectuals, reversing their long-standing contempt for the politics of "class warfare," became the most adept practitioners of that same politics, now rechristened as the "culture wars." Even notably secular writers became "image consultants for Protestant fundamentalists," Michael Lind wrote in his essay "Why Intellectual Conservatism Died," published in the quarterly *Dissent* in 1995. Lind, a onetime protégé of both Irving Kristol and William Buckley, offered a bleak *tour d'horizon* of the movement's intellectual condition in the 1990s: "In 1984, the leading conservative spokesman in the media was George Will; by 1994, it was Rush Limbaugh. The basic concerns of intellectual conservatives in the eighties were foreign policy and economics; by the early nineties they had become dirty pictures and deviant sex." They not only abandoned Burke. They had become inverse Marxists, placing loyalty to the movement above their civic responsibilities.

"As the liberties and the restrictions vary with times and circumstances, and admit of infinite modifications, they cannot be settled upon any abstract rule," Burke wrote in 1790. Ideology must subordinate itself to political reality. Contrast this formulation with Irving Kristol's celebrated observations, in 1995, on the conservative movement he helped create: "Conservatism in America is a *movement*, a popular movement, not a faction within any political party," Kristol wrote. "Though, inevitably, most conservatives vote Republican, they are not party loyalists and the party has to woo them to win their votes. This movement is issue oriented. It will happily meld with the Republican party if the party is 'right' on the issues; if not, it will walk away."

This calculus reverses Burke's. For Kristol the obligations all flow in a single direction. Parties are accountable to movement purists, while purists incur no reciprocal obligation to the party, despite its institutional authority. Kristol does not consider whether purists might be expected to modify their views or restrain their passions, for the good not only of the party but also of the broader polity—of civil society itself, the "national purpose" he once had promoted.

He now championed "religious conservatives, especially

Protestant evangelical conservatives," who discerned with unique clarity "that statism in America is organically linked with secular liberalism—that many of the programs and activities of the welfare state have a powerful antireligious bias."

It was the alliance of neoconservatives and evangelicals that formed the movement's core during the Bush years and responded most exuberantly to the administration's policies—from its "faith-based" initiatives through the war on terror and the crusading mission to "democratize" Iraq.

And by their lights, they were fully justified in doing so. Bush, so often labeled a traitor to movement principles, was in fact more steadfastly devoted to them than any of his Republican predecessors—including Reagan. Few on the right acknowledge this today, for obvious reasons. But not so long ago many did. At his peak, following September 11, Bush commanded the loyalties of every major faction of the Republican Party. The central domestic proposal of his first term, the $1.3 trillion tax cut, extended Reagan's massive "tax reform" from the 1980s. His massive Medicare prescription drug bill was in line with Reagan's continuation of Social Security and Medicare. And the huge deficits Bush amassed, though they angered small-government conservatives, had a precedent, too. As David Frum points out in *Dead Right*, "federal spending rose explosively during the golden age of Reagan." Shortly before the Iraq invasion, Martin Anderson, Reagan's top domestic policy adviser, told Bill Keller (writing in *The New York Times Magazine*) that Bush was unmistakably Reagan's heir. "On taxes, on education, it was the same. On Social Security, Bush's position was exactly what Reagan always wanted and talked about in the '70s," Anderson said. "I just can't think of any major policy issue on which Bush was different." The prime initiative of Bush's second term, the attempt to privatize Social Security, drew directly on movement scripture: Milton Friedman denounced the "compulsory annuities" of Social Security in *Capitalism and Freedom*. Buckley noted the advantages of "voluntary" accounts in his early manifesto, *Up from Liberalism*. So did Barry Goldwater during his presidential campaign in 1964. Bush went further than Reagan, too, in the war he waged against the federal bureaucracy. And his attacks on the "liberal-left bias of the major media" were the most aggressive since Nixon's.

And then there was Iraq, the event that shaped Bush's presidency and, by most accounts, brought both him and the movement to ruin. Conservatives like Buckley and Will had strong reservations, because they knew the costs of morally inspired warfare. As early as 1969, Buckley had referred, in antiquarian terms, to the "evangelistic" anti-Communism of "the old conservatives," with their "talk, even, of rolling back the Iron Curtain— the liberation rhetoric of the early fifties." Yet this liberation rhetoric was revived in 2002 as "the Bush doctrine."

The Iraq war was the event most at odds with classical conservative thinking. So indifferent to the actual requirements of civil society at home, Bush's war planners gave no serious thought to how difficult it might be to create such a society in a distant land with a vastly different history. Those within the administration who tried to make this case were marginalized or removed from power.

In one of his prescient early writings, *Vindication of the English Constitution*, a pamphlet published in 1835, the very young Disraeli reviewed the parallel democratizing experiments of his own time. In every nation where democracy had flourished, Disraeli observed, the rule of law was already embedded in social custom. This was why America had easily made the transition from a colonial protectorate to an independent constitutional society, while South American nations had not. Democracy was the fruit, not the precondition, of civil order. "Political institutions, founded on abstract rights and principles, are mere nullities," Disraeli wrote. Europe, too, had its pre-democratic places where "a comparative civilisation had been obtained under the influence of a despotic priesthood. And these are the regions to which it is thought fit suddenly to apply the institutions which regulate the civil life of Yorkshire and of Kent!"

In the end, movement conservatives got the war they wanted—at home and abroad. It was repudiated in the 2008 election, with the emergence of a president who seems more thoroughly steeped in the Burkean principles of "conservation" and "correction" than any significant thinker or political figure on the right today.

AFTERLIFE?

"I confess that I know who is a conservative less surely than I know who is a liberal," William F. Buckley wrote in 1963.

Blindfold me, spin me about like a top, and I will walk up to the single liberal in the room without zig or zag and find him even if he is hiding behind the flower pot. I am tempted to try to develop an equally sure nose for the conservative, but I am deterred by the knowledge that conservatives, under the stress of our times, have had to invite all kinds of people into their ranks to help with the job at hand, and . . . to treat such people not as janissaries, but as equals; and so, empirically, it becomes difficult to see behind the khaki, to know surely whether that is a conservative over there doing what needs to be done, or a radical, or merely a noisemaker, or pyrotechnician.

The movement has always had a disproportionate share of noisemakers and pyrotechnicians. Today they are not only more numerous than before. They seem all that's left. Classical conservatives have all either deserted the Right or been evicted from it. A striking difference between conservatism past and present is the reverse flow of intellectuals away from the movement. The converts of yesteryear—Burnham and Chambers, Moynihan and Kristol—have been succeeded by writers and thinkers like Mark Lilla and Michael Lind, Francis Fukuyama and Fareed Zakaria, David Brooks and Andrew Sullivan, who have defected in the opposite direction, fleeing the cloistered precincts of the Right. Another serious conservative journalist, David Frum, though still a loyal Republican, has lamented that "a generation of young Americans has been lost to our party."

Some see this as a triumph. The Right has been proved wrong, and that can only be good. But America needs a serious, rigorous opposition. Skeptics and outsiders perform a vital function in a democracy. It is they who ask the most uncomfortable questions, who gaze most critically at the existing arrangements of our politics and culture.

Since its founding, our nation has been productively divided between liberal and conservative impulses. They form the dialectic of our infinitely renewable politics. And there are signs of a growing debate on the right. In the first months of the Obama presidency, the moderate Republican Arnold Schwarzenegger, the governor of California, advised others in his party to do "what the people want you to do rather than getting stuck in your ideology." Florida governor Charlie Crist agreed. Another moderate Republican governor, Jon Huntsman Jr., of Utah, found he had more in common with the Obama administration than with his own party.

The "principles" Schwarzenegger rejects are still cherished by movement politicians—Haley Barbour of Mississippi, Bobby Jindal of Louisiana, Sarah Palin of Alaska, Mark Sanford of South Carolina, some of whom proudly declined the federal aid the Obama administration offered to their states. Texas's governor, Rick Perry, even talked of "seceding" from the Union, the crowning reductio ad absurdum of movement protest ostensibly undertaken in defense of American values.

These divisions reflect transformations that have little to do with the ideological debates of the past: Crist and Schwarzenegger administer populous states with diverse populations and complex global economies—microcosms of America itself. Their adversaries come from what Lind has termed the "Republiconfederacy" and what Palin infamously called "real America" and "pro-America areas"—the eroding island of movement politics. This discord reflects more than regional differences. It reflects two opposed ideas of conservatism. When Schwarzenegger calls for Republicans to discard their allegiance to "principles," he is echoing the admonitions of Disraeli. And when Sanford declares his fealty to "the basics," he means the tenets of movement faith, with its disdain both for government and for the flexible adjustments that guarantee the survival of our civil society.

What, then, should conservatives do? How can they reconnect with the country they profess to love, with the rhythms and motions of its culture, its continual acts of political self-replenishment? They might begin by considering the parallel case of liberals a generation ago, when they, too, saw their high ambitions brought precipitately to ruin but were slow to absorb the lessons of their fall from power. Even as the nation's political center had shifted, many on the left remained in thrall to "the New Politics" of the Vietnam period. They confused the programmatic inclusiveness of "identity politics" with a true majoritarianism, even as large blocs of working-class voters deserted the party.

Logic dictated another course for liberals: listening more closely to the arguments being put forth by the other side. Eventually, some did—neoliberal politicians like Gary Hart, and the editors and writers at *The New Republic*. So did Bill Clinton, who accepted the Democratic presidential nomination in 1992 "in the name of all those who do the work, pay the taxes, raise the kids and play by the rules—in the name of the hard-working Americans who make up our forgotten middle class." The language came directly from 1960s conservative tribunes—in fact, it all but plagiarized Barry Goldwater's odes to the "Forgotten American." Barack Obama made a point, during the 2008 campaign, of acknowledging the "transformational" presidency of Ronald Reagan. He has since been modeling much of his foreign policy on the careful stewardship of George H. W. Bush.

This might seem cynical—Democrats craftily co-opting or impersonating Republicans. But these acknowledgments of the Republicans' ideological victories established that liberals had learned their lessons and had also adjusted to a new, more conservative era. It certified their authority to govern.

Once again the American Right must "face historical reality," as Whittaker Chambers advised half a century ago. So tightly wedded to the politics of protest, movement ideologues have missed the most salient fact about America today: the nation has entered a conservative phase, perhaps the most conservative since the Eisenhower years. This is why Senator Arlen Specter, a longtime Republican moderate facing sure defeat in a primary campaign dominated by movement conservatives, could abruptly switch parties without altering any of his important positions. It is also why David Souter, who in his nineteen years on the Supreme Court infuriated so many on the right by his refusal to advance the movement's pet judicial causes—instead immersing himself in the study of history, partly to uncover in the past "some relevance to a constitutional rule where earlier judges saw none"—may well endure as the most authentic conservative in the Court's modern history.

And it is why attempts to depict Barack Obama as a radical or socialist dissolve under the most rudimentary examination of the facts. The decision by his team of conservative, Wall Street–inflected economists to fortify the banking system and improve the flow of credit is patently an attempt to salvage the free market, quite as the economic conservative Roosevelt tried to do in 1933. Obama's plan to extend health coverage to the nearly fifty million Americans who lack it is pure Disraeli. And Obama's foreign policy, premised on diplomacy and multilateral concord, is as forceful a repudiation of the imperial presidency as we have seen in the modern era. All these are the actions of a leader who, while politically liberal, is temperamentally conservative and who has placed his faith in the durability—and renewability—of American institutions.

Culturally, too, these are conservative times. The Right should revel in the emergence of a new generation of college students who have rediscovered the virtues of public service and volunteerism, and of business school graduates who are turning away from Wall Street, either to experiment with Internet commerce or to choose altogether different careers. What better evidence that the young are no longer alienated from our civil society and that the chasm between the "business elite" and the "adversary culture" is negotiable after all—and may someday narrow to extinction? So, too, conservatives should savor the embrace of "family values" by the nation's homosexual population, who seek the sanctuary—and responsibilities—of marriage and child-rearing, a development unthinkable a generation ago, when gays personified the excesses of the "alternative lifestyle."

All this illuminates a central truth of human nature. Most of us are liberal *and* conservative: we cling to the past in some ways, push forward into the future in others, and seek to reconcile our most cherished notions and beliefs—"prejudices" in Burke's term, "animal faith" in Santayana's—with the demands of unanticipated events. Politics is the public expression of this drama, the theater in which the modus vivendi of our civil society is continually enacted—and replenished.

What the times demand today of movement conservatives, if they are to reclaim their place at the center of American politics, is a recognition that the age of orthodoxy—of uncompromising certitude—has ended and will not be reborn anytime soon. At its best, conservatism has served the vital function of clarifying our shared connection to the past and of giving articulate voice to the shared beliefs Americans have striven to maintain under the most trying circumstances. There remains in our politics a place for an authentic conservatism—a conservatism that seeks not to destroy but to conserve.

Acknowledgments

I have spent much of my adult life as a working editor, so it is a privilege to acknowledge my gratitude to so many other editors.

At the outset of George W. Bush's presidency the peerless Leon Wieseltier, literary editor of *The New Republic*, urged me to assess—and reassess—the rise and fall of modern conservatism. The essays that resulted, plus another, "Conservatism Is Dead," commissioned by Frank Foer, the editor of *The New Republic*, and edited by Peter Scoblic, form the basis of this book.

From time to time, Robert Silvers, the editor of *The New York Review of Books,* has commissioned essays from me on Cold War anti-Communism. I have drawn on one of them, about Joseph McCarthy, in this book.

Graydon Carter and Bruce Handy, my editors at *Vanity Fair* from 1999 to 2004, encouraged me to report and write on various aspects of Bush's first term, from the role of neoconservative intellectuals to the activities of the House Republican majority. That work helped guide my efforts here.

Bob Harris, my editor and co-conspirator at *The New York Times Book Review*, and Dave Smith, my editor and co-conspirator at the Week in Review section, honed my thinking and prose on more occasions than I can count. Barry Gewen, another *Book Review* colleague, generously shared his great knowledge of modern ideology, left and right. Two other *Book Review* colleagues, Jude Biersdorfer and Nancy Martinez, came to my rescue time and again.

I also received invaluable advice from esteemed friends in book publishing, in particular Bill Thomas and Dori Weintraub.

Bob Loomis, my editor at Random House for twenty years now, is an authentic legend as well as a humbling inspiration to anyone who thinks he knows something about putting sentences together.

Three gifted researchers, Geoff Kabaservice, Jamie Kirchick, and Andrew Mangino, each supplied me in turn with rich nuggets from William F. Buckley Jr.'s papers at Yale. And as always I am indebted to Kathy and Lydia, who have steadily enriched my understanding of all manner of subjects, including the human ones that underlie the struggles and quarrels described in this book.

Select Bibliography

Arendt, Hannah. *On Revolution.* New York: Viking, 1963.

Buckley, William F., Jr. *God and Man at Yale.* Washington, D.C.: Regnery, 1977 (paperback reprint, orig. 1951).

————. *The Governor Listeth: A Book of Inspired Political Revelations.* New York: Berkley, 1971 (paperback reprint, orig. 1970).

————. *The Jeweler's Eye.* New York: Berkley, 1969 (paperback reprint, orig. 1968).

————. *Rumbles Left and Right: A Book About Troublesome People and Ideas.* New York: McFadden-Bartell, 1964 (paperback reprint, orig. 1963).

————, ed. *American Conservative Thought in the Twentieth Century.* Indianapolis: Bobbs-Merrill, 1970.

———— and L. Brent Bozell. *McCarthy and His Enemies: The Record and Its Meaning.* Washington, D.C.: Regnery, 1995 (paperback reprint, orig. 1961).

Burke, Edmund. *Reflections on the Revolution in France.* New York: MacMillan, 1955 (paperback reprint, orig. 1790).

Burnham, James. *Congress and the American Tradition.* Chicago: Regnery, 1965 (reprint, orig. 1959).

——. *The Managerial Revolution.* Bloomington, Ind.: Indiana University Press, 1966 (paperback reprint, orig. 1941).

Chambers, Whittaker. *Ghosts on the Roof: Selected Journalism of Whittaker Chambers, 1931–1959.* Ed. Terry Teachout. Washington, D.C.: Regnery, 1989.

——. *Odyssey of a Friend: Whittaker Chambers' Letters to William F. Buckley, Jr., 1954–1961.* Ed. William F. Buckley Jr. New York: Putnam, 1969.

Disraeli, Benjamin. *Selected Speeches.* New York: Elibron Classics, 2005 (paperback reprint, orig. 1904).

Hofstadter, Richard. *The Paranoid Style in American Politics and Other Essays.* New York: Vintage, 1967 (paperback reprint, orig. 1965).

Kendall, Willmoore. *Willmoore Kendall Contra Mundum.* Ed. Nellie Kendall. Lanham, Md.: University Press of America, 1994 (paperback reprint, orig. 1971).

Kristol, Irving. *Neoconservatism: The Autobiography of an Idea.* Chicago: Ivan R. Dee, 1999 (paperback reprint, orig. 1995).

Lubell, Samuel. *The Future of American Politics.* New York: Harper and Brothers, 1952.

Mencken, H. L. *H. L. Mencken on Politics: A Carnival of Buncombe.* Ed. Malcolm Moos. Baltimore: Johns Hopkins University Press, 1996 (paperback reprint, orig. 1956).

Phillips, Kevin. *The Emerging Republican Majority.* New Rochelle, N.Y.: Arlington House, 1969.

Rainwater, Lee, and William L. Yancey. *The Moynihan Report and the Politics of Controversy.* Cambridge, Mass.: MIT Press (paperback), 1967.

Rovere, Richard H. *Affairs of State, 1950–1956: The Eisenhower Years.* New York: Farrar, Straus and Cudahy, 1956.

White, Theodore H. *The Making of the President, 1972.* New York: Atheneum, 1973.

———. *Theodore H. White at Large: The Best of His Magazine Writing, 1939–1986.* Ed. Edward T. Thompson. New York: Pantheon, 1992.

Will, George F. *Statecraft as Soulcraft: What Government Does.* New York: Touchstone, 1984 (paperback reprint, orig. 1983).

Wills, Garry. *Confessions of a Conservative.* New York: Doubleday, 1979.

———. *Nixon Agonistes: The Crisis of the Self-Made Man.* Boston: Houghton Mifflin, 1970.

ABOUT THE AUTHOR

SAM TANENHAUS is the editor of both *The New York Times Book Review* and the Week in Review section of the *Times*. From 1999 to 2004 he was a contributing editor at *Vanity Fair*, where he wrote often on politics. His work has also appeared in *The New York Times Magazine, The New Republic, The New York Review of Books,* and many other publications. Tanenhaus's previous book, *Whittaker Chambers: A Biography,* won the *Los Angeles Times* Book Prize and was a finalist for both the National Book Award and the Pulitzer Prize.

This book was set in Monotype Dante, a typeface designed by Giovanni Mardersteig (1892–1977). Conceived as a private type for the Officina Bodoni in Verona, Italy, Dante was originally cut only for hand composition by Charles Malin, the famous Parisian punch cutter, between 1946 and 1952. Its first use was in an edition of Boccaccio's *Trattetello in laude di Dante* that appeared in 1954. The Monotype Corporation's version of Dante followed in 1957. Though modeled on the Aldine type used for Pietro Cardinal Bembo's treatise *De Aetna* in 1495, Dante is a thoroughly modern interpretation of that venerable face.